The Recent Unpleasantness

To Patience and Laure with best wishes —

The Recent
Unpleasantness

Calvary Church's Role in the Preservation of the
Episcopal Church in the Diocese of Pittsburgh

HAROLD T. LEWIS

FOREWORD BY
MARK HOLLINGSWORTH

WIPF & STOCK · Eugene, Oregon

Wipf & Stock
An Imprint of Wipf and Stock Publishers
199 W. 8th Ave., Suite 3
Eugene, OR 97401

www.wipfandstock.com

ISBN 13: 978-1-4982-0482-8

Manufactured in the U.S.A.

To Claudette

Contents

Acknowledgments

WE EXPRESS OUR SINCERE appreciation to all those persons who lent us their assistance.

In the parish, to all the members of the Vestry who served during this challenging period in the life of the congregation and diocese, especially Philip R. Roberts, senior warden and plaintiff; and Gordon D. Fisher, Esq., junior warden. We acknowledge the invaluable assistance of Walter P. DeForest III, Esq., Calvary's attorney, and the members of his firm; and Charles B. Jarrett Jr., Esq., a member of the parish and former chancellor of the diocese.

In the Diocese of Pittsburgh, we acknowledge the support of Progressive Episcopalians of Pittsburgh (PEP) and its officers, Lionel Deimel, Joan Gundersen, and Mary Roehrich, especially for their efforts in bringing together diverse groups within the diocese, and for educating members of the diocese about the nature of the problems we endured and how those problems related to challenges faced by fellow Christians throughout the Episcopal Church and the Anglican Communion. We thank Rev. Diane Shepard, rector, and the vestry of St. Stephen's, Wilkinsburg; and Mr. Herman ("Bud") Harvey of S. Stephen's, Sewickley, who joined Calvary in the lawsuit. We also recognize the indefatigable efforts of Andrew Roman, Esq., diocesan chancellor. We are especially grateful to the Rev. Dr. James B. Simons, rector of St. Michael's-in-the-Valley, Ligonier, who was largely responsible for reorganizing the standing committee and restoring the structure of the diocese after the 2008 diocesan convention.

ACKNOWLEDGMENTS

In the broader Episcopal Church, we express gratitude to the Most Reverend Katharine Jefferts Schori, presiding bishop and primate, for her unstinting support, and for the timely assistance rendered by her chancellor, David Booth Beers, Esq., and his associate Mary Kostel, Esq. We are indebted as well to Bishops Mark Hollingsworth, Stacey Sauls, and William Swing of the House of Bishops Committee on Property Matters; and Michael Glass, Esq., a lawyer from the Diocese of San Joaquin, later its chancellor. Finally, we thank those individuals and parishes throughout the Church who made contributions to the legal fund, especially congregations of the Consortium of Endowed Episcopal Parishes.

Pittsburgh, SS. Philip & James, May 1, 2014

Foreword

THE INSTITUTIONAL CHURCH MAY well seem from the outside to be a sometime odd institution. Many expect that denominations are made up of like-minded believers, birds of a feather flocking together. While this may be so in the occasional individual congregation, mainline churches, in both parochial and denominational contexts, reflect quite a different dynamic. It seems that in them God calls together people of differing convictions, often quite unlikely companions, in the divine expectation that they come not to a common mind but to a common heart. It appears God's intention that, in becoming one body, they learn how to live together in spite of and enriched by all their differences, in genuine compassion and selfless advocacy for the other, and thereby witness to a world desperate for models of how to live together in peace.

The struggles of the Episcopal Church have consistently borne this out, from its formation in the wake of the Revolutionary War, through its divisions in the American Civil War, to today. Presenting issues have included racial equality, the leadership of women, liturgical expression and language, biblical interpretation, and, most recently, human sexuality. But at the core is always the age-old struggle for power—who gets to define orthodoxy, who gets to dictate who is in and who is out.

In *The Recent Unpleasantness*, the Rev. Dr. Harold T. Lewis has chronicled the Episcopal Church's latest experience of this timeless battle, from a perspective as close as anyone's in the Church. As rector of Calvary Church, Pittsburgh, he became a point person at the epicenter of this division in both the Episcopal Church and the Anglican Communion, as he and his parishioners fought for the unity of the Body of Christ and for accountability within the Diocese of Pittsburgh and from its bishop.

With characteristic clarity and humility, Dr. Lewis offers us a firsthand account of the theological, ecclesiastical, and legal wrangling of a house divided locally and internationally. Both scholarly and eminently accessible, the book serves as a primer in Episcopal Church polity and canonical structure, as well as it explicates insightfully the complicated relational dynamics of the Anglican Communion.

The Recent Unpleasantness exposes Harold Lewis once again as a gifted historian and incisive ecclesiologist, and history itself will doubtless record him as a courageous hero of the church. It is a privilege to have served with him in that difficult season and now.

The Rt. Rev. Mark Hollingsworth Jr.
Bishop of Ohio
Season after Pentecost 2014

Introduction

"Meiosis"

EARLY ON IN THE dispute between Calvary Episcopal Church in Pittsburgh and the Rt. Rev. Robert William Duncan, seventh bishop of Pittsburgh, we referred to the conflict in which we were engaged as "the recent unpleasantness." It was an apt description, but we did not coin the phrase. It had been an expression long used, especially in the South, as a euphemistic description of the Civil War and its aftermath. It is not an exaggeration to compare our local conflict, which was in many ways a microcosm of the discord that existed in the broader church, to the Civil War. Ours was, when all is said and done, an internecine struggle between two factions within the church, the Body of Christ. Like the nation torn asunder a century and a half ago, the Episcopal Church was (and some would say, still is), to borrow a phrase that President Lincoln borrowed, in turn, from the Gospel of Matthew (12:26), "a house divided against itself." Too, it is clear that, like the nation that found itself pitched in battle in the mid-nineteenth century, we were divided by ideology and theology. Differences at the time of the Civil War centered around the nefarious institution of slavery; differences in the more recent struggle focused on a plethora of social and theological issues, including, but by no means limited to, the issue of human sexuality.

The most obvious similarity, of course, is that a secession took place in both instances. American history tells of the formation of the Confederate States of America and, interestingly enough, the Confederate Episcopal Church, the latter made up of dioceses in slaveholding states.[1] It should be noted that "secession" is not a word to be found in any documents, speeches, sermons, or other communications that emanated from the offices of Bishop Duncan, by others who espoused a separation, or by the groups spawned by them. They would maintain that their new church organizations most often came into being as a result of something called "realignment," not "secession." But we are reminded of the adage, "If you call a horse a noble steed, it is still a fine horse."

That said, we should make it clear at the outset that when in the following pages we refer to the secession on the part of Bishop Duncan and his followers, we are referring to a de facto separation along theological and ideological lines, not to a legal or canonical occurrence. The reason is that such an official action is not possible under church law. While individuals are clearly free to leave one church body and join another, dioceses, creatures of the General Convention of the Episcopal Church, and parishes, which are created by dioceses, are not free to separate or secede from their respective parent bodies. An understanding of this principle of canon law is essential in order to comprehend the legal justification for our lawsuit.

In the recent conflict, therefore, a secession of persons, not dioceses, resulted in the establishment of, *inter alia*, the self-styled

1. One of the long-held myths of the Episcopal Church is that it is the sole denomination that never split over the slavery issue. But in fact the admittedly short-lived Confederate Episcopal Church was founded and organized in 1862. Northern Episcopalians refused to recognize the secession and as a result the Episcopal Church never acknowledged the existence of the Confederate Episcopal Church, which faded into oblivion after the end of the war. (see Lewis, *Yet with a Steady Beat*, 44.) It is noteworthy that Bishop Duncan, at the diocesan convention in 2007, cited the formation of the Confederate Episcopal Church as justification for the secession of the Diocese of Pittsburgh from the Episcopal Church. His argument was that when the Confederate states withdrew from TEC, TEC did not enact a canon or constitutional change asserting that such an action was illegal. In other words, the bishop interpreted the church's silence as assent, thereby giving carte blanche to all dioceses, in perpetuity, to separate themselves from TEC, despite their constitutional obligation to remain in communion with it.

Anglican Church in North America, whose first archbishop was, not surprisingly, Robert Duncan. Although ACNA had the "trappings" of a province of the Anglican Communion,[2] it was never recognized as such by the Anglican Consultative Council (ACC)[3] or the Archbishop of Canterbury.[4] Before the formation of ACNA, however, the Diocese of Pittsburgh sought and received permission from the Province of the Southern Cone, a province of the Anglican Church made up of the dioceses in Argentina, Bolivia, Chile, Peru, Paraguay, and Uruguay, to be affiliated with it—and indeed, the Southern Cone became its temporary resting place when the schism in the Diocese of Pittsburgh occurred in 2008, at which time clergy in the diocese received a certificate officially informing all of them, whether they had voted for "realignment" or not, that they were as of that date canonically resident in the Province of the Southern Cone!

It must be underscored that the coming into being of ACNA or the "grafting" of the Diocese of Pittsburgh onto an extant province in South America constitutes a concept that is novel to Anglicanism. Dioceses and provinces have long been geographically contiguous entities, containing "all sorts and conditions" of men

2. The Anglican Communion, the third largest Christian body in the world, has approximately eighty million members around the globe. It is made up of geographical groupings called provinces, each of which contains four or more dioceses, each diocese being a geographical entity under the authority of a local bishop.

3. The Anglican Consultative Council, made up of one to three members of each of the forty or so provinces of the Communion, is primarily responsible for advising the Communion on its structures and organization, and developing common policies for the implementation of the work of the Communion. The ACC's policy on new ecclesiastical jurisdictions, as delineated in its third and tenth gatherings, is that such jurisdictions could take place as a result of a "clear transfer of metropolitical authority," not unilateral in action.

4. The Archbishop of Canterbury has no official jurisdiction outside of the Church of England, but as *primus inter pares* ("first among equals") is recognized as the spiritual leader of the worldwide Anglican Communion. He is one of the four "instruments of unity" of Anglicanism, the others being: the Lambeth Conference, the decennial gathering of all Anglican bishops; the Primates' Meeting, made up of the heads (normally archbishops) of each of the provinces; and the Anglican Consultative Council.

and women. The idea that provinces and dioceses can be made up of ideologically determined components, a process that would result in "parallel" or overlapping jurisdictions, runs counter to the historic catholicity that Robert Duncan and his followers claimed to uphold and defend.[5]

Duncan, nevertheless, boldly invented a new theological principle. In a speech on the future of Anglicanism, he declared, "Diocesan boundaries are lost forever, at least in the United States," and then proceeded to lay the blame for that development not on the willful actions of the conservative wing of the church, but rather on the "resistance by American progressives to early suggestions of ways to accommodate conservatives in progressive dioceses." Suggesting that the overturning of a universally accepted system of autonomous, geographically based dioceses and its replacement by ideologically determined factions was little more than an inevitable developmental process, Duncan added: "The embrace of affinity relationships, rather than geographical location, as the organizing principle of the Anglican Mission in America,[6] has also *offered an intentional alternative to classic assumptions about diocesan structure. Things will never return to the simplicity of one Anglican bishop having authority over one Anglican territory.*"[7]

"Recent unpleasantness" is an example, rhetoricians tell us, of a meiosis. From a Greek word meaning to diminish or make smaller, meiosis is "a euphemistic figure of speech that intentionally understates something or implies that it is lesser in significance or size than it really is." (A familiar example would be referring to the Atlantic Ocean as "the Pond.") Our quasi-jocular use of the term, however, was never meant to belittle or minimize in any way the gravity of the situation. In fact, psychologists might suggest that its use was a way to lessen the painful reality of what was going

5. Parallel jurisdictions were condemned by the Council of Nicaea (325) and by successive Lambeth Conferences from 1878 to the present.

6. The Anglican Mission in America (AMiA), since renamed the Anglican Mission in the Americas, was founded in 2000 under the auspices of the Province of Rwanda. A breakaway Anglican church, its purpose was to provide "oversight" for disaffected Episcopalians in the U.S.

7. Duncan, "Future of Anglicanism," italics added.

on. Bishop Duncan and his supporters not infrequently accused us of a variety of ulterior motives for our actions—suggesting that they amounted to a power play, or that they were products of self-aggrandizement, a lack of grounding in biblical or Christian principles, animosity between the bishop and the rector of Calvary Church, or just plain mean-spiritedness. Indeed, as Steve Levin, religion editor for the *Pittsburgh Post-Gazette*, accurately reported, we were regarded "as pariahs in a diocese overwhelmingly supportive of its bishop and his ongoing leadership of a network of biblically conservative dioceses unhappy with the direction of the national church and eager to gain acceptance as the 'true' Anglican Church in the eyes of the worldwide Anglican Communion."[8]

It is important to remember, therefore, that we were always deeply sensible of the pain and discomfort involved in taking such actions as suing our bishop in open court, and eventually signing a document requesting that he be deposed from the ministry of the church. To borrow a phrase from the marriage service in the 1928 *Book of Common Prayer*, we did no enter into these actions "unadvisedly or lightly, but reverently, discreetly, advisably, soberly, and in the fear of God."

---

8. Levin, "Rector Criticizes Prevailing Conservatism."

1

Portents

2003 IS THE FOCAL point of the intriguing drama that unfolded in the Diocese of Pittsburgh. It was in that year that the General Convention approved the ordination and consecration of V. Gene Robinson. It was also the year in which the bishop and board of trustees of the Diocese of Pittsburgh took steps that portended attempts at separation from the Episcopal Church; and that the diocesan convention passed resolutions in the hopes of effecting that plan. It was in that year that Calvary Episcopal Church of Pittsburgh filed suit in civil court to prevent its being carried out. But the story does not begin there. Jesus said, "Unless you see signs and wonders you will not believe" (John 4:48). There were several such signs and wonders, portents along the way, literally decades in the making, that led to this unprecedented chain of events.

TESM: THE "E" IS SILENT

Among the first of these is the founding, in 1976, of Trinity Episcopal School for Ministry (TESM),[1] an institution whose presence,

1. A long-standing joke was that the "E" in TESM was silent. This became official in 2007, when "Episcopal" was dropped from the Seminary's publications and printed materials, reflecting the fact that many, indeed most, of its

arguably, has had a greater effect on the life, ethos, theology, and politics of the Diocese of Pittsburgh than any other entity, internal or external to its existence. Trinity's founders, many of whom had been influenced by the charismatic movement, believed that the Episcopal Church (TEC) had been swept away by a rampant liberal theology and its concomitant secular relativism. In their opinion, TEC had ignored the Pauline admonition "not to conform to this world but be transformed by the renewal of your mind" (Rom 12:2). The founders sought to establish a theological institution based on orthodox Protestant theology and evangelical principles.

When the site chosen for the seminary turned out to be within the boundaries of the Episcopal Diocese of Pittsburgh, permission of the bishop had to be obtained. Robert Appleyard, fifth bishop of Pittsburgh (1968–1982) was not at all sympathetic to the theological bent of the proposed school. He was a liberal, catholic churchman, known for his passion for racial justice, his commitment to urban ministry, and for his championing of women's rights.[2] Although advised by many to withhold his permission for Trinity to be planted in his diocese, he decided to grant the permission nevertheless, believing that the large tent of Anglicanism was commodious enough to embrace the theological diversity that Trinity would undoubtedly bring.[3]

students came from dioceses in breakaway Anglican communities, such as the Anglican Church in North America (ACNA), the Anglican Mission in the Americas (AMiA), and other "realigned" churches. Trinity Episcopal School for Ministry has been retained, however, as its corporate and legal name, perhaps so that it would remain eligible for certain funding and scholarships and other benefits from national Episcopal bodies.

2. Beryl Choi, the first woman priest in the Diocese of Pittsburgh, and one of the first in the EC, was ordained by Bishop Appleyard in 1977, and served as an assistant priest at Calvary Church.

3 At the time of Appleyard's episcopate, most people believed, as one wag described it, that the Episcopal Church was made up of three components: the low and lazy, the broad and hazy, and the high and crazy; that is to say, liturgical minimalists, the middle-of-the-road types, and the Anglo-Catholic eccentrics—these groups representing theological views ranging from Protestant/evangelical to staunch traditionalists. At that time, however, each group, despite its personal preferences and "brand" of theology, regarded the other groups with respect and as full members of the same church. There was a

TESM, as it grew, depended largely on four groups to make up its student body, the first three of these being ordinands from the Diocese of Pittsburgh, ordinands sent by Episcopal bishops who shared TESM's theological views and its vision for the church, and so-called "orthodox" students, many of whom had been denied access to the ordination process in their respective mainstream dioceses in TEC, and who, upon their arrival in Pittsburgh, were placed on a "fast track" to enable them to be ordained in that diocese. (This involved "adoption" by a local parish, whose rector and vestry would sponsor them and provide the necessary approvals throughout the ordination process.) The fourth group must not be overlooked. It was made up of students from overseas, especially from conservative, evangelical dioceses in Africa. Although such students normally returned to their home dioceses upon graduation, they maintained close ties with the Diocese of Pittsburgh, and formed staunch alliances with conservative Episcopalians in the United States. Indeed, Bishop Duncan wrote of his participation in the 1998 Lambeth Conference, "The impact of TSM on the global scene is vast. I met bishops from every continent who were trained at or who have been connected to this twenty-year-old institution."

It should be further pointed out that because TESM graduates, owing to their theological conservatism, often had limited placement opportunities in the broader church, many of them were deployed in the Diocese of Pittsburgh, where TESM alumni had begun to establish a foothold, resulting in a situation in which the theological climate, especially during the tenure of Alden Hathaway (who succeeded Appleyard as bishop, 1982–1997), steadily and inexorably moved well to the right of center. As Joan Gundersen observes in her history of the diocese:

> Trinity School for Ministry became a magnet for evangelicals and during Appleyard's administration the diocese became more contentious . . . The Brotherhood of St. Andrew, Church Army, Community of Celebration,

---

complete absence of derision or contempt for other groups or any evidence that one group believed another to be somehow less than legitimate.

Episcopal Church Missionary Community and South American Missionary Society and other [conservative] groups began making Pittsburgh their headquarters. By the time of Alden Hathaway's consecration in 1982, evangelicals were strong enough to begin reshaping the diocese.[4]

This, in turn, was reflected in the ethos of the congregations served by TESM graduates, but had its most profound effect on the votes cast at diocesan conventions. By the time Robert Duncan assumed the helm,[5] he could depend on the support of easily two thirds of the clergy and lay delegates to the diocesan convention to support his initiatives. This percentage increased to roughly three fourths through the "planning" of several fledgling congregations.

The "signs and wonders" on which I will concentrate, however, begin with the events in 1996, the year in which Robert Duncan was consecrated to succeed Alden Hathaway as seventh bishop of Pittsburgh, and in which I was instituted as fifteenth rector of Calvary Church. The portents were, in effect, actions that served to distance the Diocese of Pittsburgh from the polity and practices of the national church and the General Convention, as regards governance, operations, ministry lay and ordained, theological positions, and fiscal management. It is worthy of note that virtually all statements issued by the bishop's office, the diocesan convention, the standing committee, and other diocesan entities espousing such separation were challenged, in writing and on the floor of diocesan conventions, by the rector and/or vestry of Calvary Church, or, in the case of diocesan conventions, clergy and

4. Gundersen, "History of the Episcopal Church in the Diocese of Pittsburgh," 4.

5. The diocesan nominating committee, charged with presenting a slate of candidates for the bishopric of Pittsburgh, considered Robert Duncan, who at the time was the canon to the ordinary (executive assistant to the diocesan bishop), but did not include him among their list of nominees. While the details of the nominating committee's process were not revealed, it was stated that Duncan did not meet the criteria that the committee had established. At the electing convention, held in 1995, after the slate was presented, Canon Duncan was nominated from the floor (a process no longer allowed in the Diocese of Pittsburgh or any other diocese) and was elected on the third ballot.

lay delegates. The following paragraphs are not intended to be an exhaustive list of occurrences, but a series of vignettes, as it were, intended to convey the overall thrust of Bishop Duncan's actions before matters came to a head at the diocesan conventions of 2003.

DIVERSION OF FUNDS

One of the first such signs of dissociation from the mainstream of the Episcopal Church was a resolution passed at the 131st diocesan convention held in November 1996 that made it possible for congregations to divert to other missionary purposes funds normally earmarked for support of the national church. It was tantamount to a vote of no confidence in the leadership of the Episcopal Church, whose presiding bishop at the time was Edmond Lee Browning, who declared upon his election in 1985 that there would be no outcasts in the Episcopal Church. Although unable to vote in the convention, having been a priest of the diocese for less than three months, I exercised my right to voice, and spoke against the resolution, arguing that the resolution ran counter to catholic principles, and that it could well be the beginning of a slippery slope as regards our relationship with the national church. We would learn in due course what a slippery slope it was. A decade later, the diocesan leadership requested "alternative primatial oversight" because they no longer recognized the authority of the presiding bishop, Katharine Jefferts Schori.

ALPHABET SOUP: THE EMERGENCE OF BREAKAWAY CHURCH ORGANIZATIONS

It is especially noteworthy for those who believe that the secession movement was occasioned by Gene Robinson's election and consecration in 2003 to point out that Bishop Duncan, within months of his own consecration in 1996, was instrumental in establishing the American Anglican Council (AAC). Made up of theologically conservative congregations and dioceses; provinces including

Nigeria, Rwanda, and the aforementioned Southern Cone; and various associations such as Forward in Faith and the Federation of Anglican Churches in the Americas, AAC saw itself as "a group which affirmed biblical authority and Christian orthodoxy,[6] whose mission was to oppose what it perceived as moral relativism in its various forms. As regards its status, it described itself as "a free-standing orthodox Anglican advocacy organization, neither in nor out of TEC, but entirely separate from it." Duncan also helped to found in 2007 the Common Cause Council of Bishops, as a "separate ecclesiastical structure in North America." Thus, the "slippery slope" toward secession continued to follow its inexorable course.

SEXUAL PROSCRIPTIONS
AND "GODLY DIRECTIONS"

It was in October 1996 that Bishops Hathaway and Duncan, at that time the diocesan and coadjutor bishops of Pittsburgh respectively, issued a pastoral letter on the subject of human sexuality. It was occasioned by the decision handed down in the 1996 heresy trial of the Rt. Rev. Walter C. Righter, retired bishop of Iowa and assisting bishop in the Diocese of Newark, who, it should be noted, had begun his ministry in the Diocese of Pittsburgh. While in Newark, acting on behalf of the diocesan bishop, John Shelby Spong, he had ordained to the diaconate a gay man who was in a committed relationship, on account of which action Bishop Righter was tried by a court made up of nine members of the House of Bishops. The court concluded that there was nothing in the core doctrine of the Episcopal Church that restrained restrain a bishop from ordaining

6. One of the disturbing developments of the so-called "realignment" movement in the Episcopal Church is its novel use of such terms as "Anglican" and "orthodox." All Episcopalians, as is the case with all members of the Anglican Communion, are Anglicans, but the "realigners" have equated "Anglicanism" with the true faith, and "Episcopalianism" with those whom they have deemed to be progressive, dissident, revisionist, and even apostate. Likewise, the term "orthodox," which comes from the Greek for "right teaching," has presumptuously been commandeered by the breakaway groups, implicitly relegating Episcopalians to the ranks of heresy.

persons living in committed same-gender relationships. Bishops Hathaway and Duncan, however, took exception to the decision, and in a joint pastoral letter, alluding to what they described as the "confusion" caused by the verdict, appealed to Holy Scripture, the Articles of Religion, and the *Book of Common Prayer*. The letter contained a "godly direction" to their clergy, and emphasized that genital sexual expression, for clergy and laypersons, is limited to relationships between men and women in marriage, and that those who are single are bound to practice abstinence. Moreover, they admonished, there should be nothing in the teaching or behavior of the clergy that could be construed to convey the acceptability of any other theological position.

In a letter dated June 9, 1997, the clergy and vestry of Calvary Church responded to the bishops in an open letter, in which they stated that they regretted that, at a time in which "church leaders have urged all Episcopalians to engage in prayerful dialogue around the issue," their pastoral letter "peremptorily cuts off discussion and would suggest that further thinking on the matter is neither desirable nor helpful for the soul's health of our church." The letter also pointed out that the bishops' statement was in direct contradiction to the decision of the General Convention "that the bishops and deputies work to establish within their respective jurisdictions the means to encourage and enable the widest possible study and conversation on the subject of homosexuality."[7] The reaction to our letter was noteworthy. One parish sent a letter to the bishops endorsing our position, adding that the diocesan stance on the issue sent "a clear message that while persons of homosexual orientation may be finding a voice in this society as the barriers to their full inclusion continue to crumble, they are not finding a welcome in our congregations, except as suspect sinners who are in particular need of repentance."[8] And while there were a few other predictably sympathetic voices, communications received by the rector and vestry of Calvary Church, by a wide margin, criticized us not only for what they deemed to be our suspect theology, but

7. Lewis et al., "Open Letter," June 9, 1997.
8. Wood, "Open Letter," July 8, 1997.

for daring to question the inspired and informed opinion of our fathers-in-God.

NATIONAL ORDINATION EXAMS: VERBOTEN?

In March of 1998, the Commission on Ministry of the Diocese of Pittsburgh, that body responsible for shepherding persons through the ordination process, announced that it would remove from the list of ordination requirements the rule that ordinands be required to take the General Ordination Examinations (GOEs). The reasons cited were that the exams were considered flawed and inadequate, both in terms of questions asked and in the method of evaluating answers. At the time, I served as an examining chaplain in homiletics for the diocese, and I wrote to the bishop resigning from that position, citing the fact that as a member of the General Board of Examining Chaplains, the national body responsible for setting and marking the GOEs, my continued participation as a diocesan examining chaplain would constitute a conflict of interest, as it would suggest that I concur with the diocesan assessment of the national examination process. I added that the recent diocesan action sent the message that the Diocese of Pittsburgh wished to distance itself from the policies and practice of the national Episcopal Church.

Bishop Duncan responded to my letter, urging me to reconsider my decision, maintaining that it was not his intention to send such a message. I cite my answer to him here, as it speaks to the "preponderance of evidence" that was emerging from seemingly disparate actions on the part of the bishop—actions that, when taken together, in my opinion, pointed clearly to his intention to effect a schism in the diocese:

> Taken in isolation, this decision [on the ordination examinations] would not necessarily lead to such a conclusion. But when seen in conjunction with the diocesan decision to authorize withholding of funds from the national church; . . . your decision to absent yourself from the Investiture of Presiding Bishop Griswold; and

your membership on the board of the American Anglican Council; you will allow that we have reason to be concerned about how this diocese sees itself in connection with the national church. Moreover, while you may have seen the decision to remove the GOE requirement as based simply on a desire to have the ordinands examined only once, it is clear that other facts were taken into consideration, specifically the contention that the GOEs are flawed. Further, one cannot help but wonder if there is some connection between this decision and a proposal discussed at a meeting of the Commission on Ministry and elsewhere to establish a "parallel" commission on ministry system to help ensure the ordination of "orthodox" candidates who have found difficulty in the ordination process in certain dioceses.[9]

INTERCONTINENTAL BALLISTIC MISSILES?

The consecrations of bishops for the Anglican Mission in America in 2000 and 2001 constituted another significant portent. They took place in Singapore and Denver respectively (the latter without the permission of the presiding bishop or the Bishop of Colorado). The AMiA, believing that TEC had lost its claim to orthodoxy, declared that it found it necessary to elevate bishops who would, in effect, do missionary work among the alleged faithful remnant in the Episcopal Church who had rejected the church's teaching. These newly mitered leaders were not recognized by the Archbishop of Canterbury, the Anglican Consultative Council, or the presiding bishop. George Carey, Archbishop of Canterbury, commenting that these consecrations were "at best, highly irregular, and at worst, simply schismatic," opined that they would cause confusion and bring scandal to our Communion.[10] Michael Peers,

9. Lewis, letter to the Rt. Rev. Robert William Duncan, April 22, 1998.

10. "Consecrations Harmful to Unity," 14. Allowing for the technical validity of the consecrations because the consecrators were in the historic succession, *The Living Church* article added that "the way their consecrations came about makes their Episcopal ministries highly suspect."

Primate of Canada and president of the Primates' Standing Committee, made a particularly insightful and cogent comment:

> In the Anglican tradition, bishops are chosen by the local church according to its standards and practices. The persons chosen are affirmed by the wider church, that is, the province, and then ordained by bishops acting in, with and for the church of the diocese and province. Bishops are not intercontinental ballistic missiles, manufactured on one continent and fired into another as an act of aggression. The recent irregular ordination in Singapore is, in my opinion, an open and premeditated assault on Anglican tradition, catholic order and Christian charity.[11]

These consecrations had a particular impact on the Diocese of Pittsburgh because some of the consecrating bishops (notably Archbishop Emmanuel Kolini) were from the Province of Rwanda, with which Pittsburgh enjoyed a companion relationship, and also because one of the newly consecrated bishops was John Rodgers, retired dean of TESM, who in his new ministry had the unbridled support of Bishop Duncan. In what we knew would be an exercise in futility, the Calvary delegation to the diocesan convention presented a resolution that the diocese terminate its relationship with Rwanda. This attempt fell on deaf ears, as Bishop Duncan saw no problem with the consecrations, referring to them as part of "a spiral of events that is testing the fabric and direction of the Church." He further described the consecrations as merely the result of efforts on his part and that of others to "provide room" for those who disagreed with the teachings of TEC.

THE TAJ MAHAL IN DONEGAL

Yet another portent was the bishop's (failed) attempt to launch a capital campaign, a large portion of whose proceeds would be used to erect a "common life center" for the diocese in Donegal, about fifty miles to the southeast of Pittsburgh (its $20-million

---

11. Peers, "Canada: Statement," February 8, 2000.

price tag led many to refer to it as the Taj Mahal)! Many of us were wary of the purposes for which the center would be built, especially since it was the bishop's stated wish that it would "develop leadership potential in the worldwide Anglican Communion." We believed that such a statement could only be interpreted in light of the role which Bishop Duncan had been playing in the Anglican Communion, and the theology that informed that role, namely, an increasing association with dioceses and provinces that had distanced themselves from the actions, decisions, and theology of TEC. Together with such dissident Anglicans, it was Bishop Duncan's expressed intent to "work assiduously to bring the Episcopal Church in our country back to its senses." Those who deemed such efforts as unnecessary could not support the idea of the common life center. It was clear to us that such a center, far from serving to bring members of a divided diocese together, as had been claimed, would instead, in our opinion, become nothing less than a headquarters for the movement within Anglicanism in which the Bishop of Pittsburgh had been so vocal and visible a champion. For these and other reasons, Calvary notified the bishop that it would not participate in the diocesan capital campaign.[12]

A BISHOP WITH A "DOMESTIC" PORTFOLIO?

To add insult to injury, Duncan proposed that the diocese support the appointment of an assistant bishop, whose responsibility would be to concentrate on matters closer to home, while the diocesan bishop continued to network with conservative Anglican colleagues abroad. Although the Common Life Center never came to fruition,[13] the bishop did prevail in appointing, through unex-

12. Despite receiving such notification from the rector and vestry, members of the diocesan Capital Campaign Committee made direct contact to several prominent parishioners, seeking their financial support. Those parishioners, aware of the parish's official decision and the reasons for having reached it, declined to lend assistance to the project.

13. Two lesser structures did come into existence on the diocesan property in Donegal. The first was a small retreat house, suitable for clergy meetings or as a weekend getaway for a clergy family. The second was the Bishop's House,

plained sources of funding, an assistant bishop in the person of the Rt. Rev. Henry Scriven, an Englishman, who had previously served as bishop suffragan of the Diocese of Europe.[14] Bishop Scriven, by all reports the more affable of the two bishops, was clearly the "good cop" to Duncan's "bad cop." He came across in parish visitations and other public appearances as if his job were to assure the members of the diocese that the situation in which we found ourselves was well within the parameters of normalcy. He was given to use his Englishness as a basis for not being aware of the intricacies of the structure of the Episcopal Church. Too, he often talked about the joy of his experience of working in the Diocese of Europe alongside other Anglican jurisdictions, the inference being that TEC could enjoy such salubrious relations with "realigned" churches should they turn out to be TEC's neighbors. Such a contention, of course, ignored the fact that, unlike the situation in Europe, there would be serious doctrinal differences between TEC and the "realigned" churches, which would have come into existence as a result of schism and not geographical accident. Scriven also contended that "orthodox" Episcopalians had no agenda, and were simply biding their time until such time as the Archbishop of Canterbury reached some conclusion as to their status. He continued to make such statements even after the line between Duncan's "two churches" and "two gospels" had been drawn in the sand by subsequent diocesan conventions!

"FIREWALL!"

Perhaps the most startling of the portents related to the diocesan convention of 2002. In his letter to the diocese in anticipation of

---

to which Robert Duncan and his wife hold life tenancy. Upon their deaths, it reverts to the Diocese of Pittsburgh.

14. Previously known as the Diocese of Fulham and Gibraltar, the Diocese of Europe is a group of Anglican parishes, administered by the Church of England, scattered throughout the continent. The Diocese was founded to minister primarily to the British expatriate community, but has since expanded its ministry.

that gathering, Bishop Duncan, using "we/they" language that had become commonplace in his communications, first reported on the failure of the capital campaign, and attributed it, in a not-too-veiled reference to Calvary Church, to "non-interest among some who used to travel with us, and alienation among some others who *perceive* that their voices are not heard."[15] He then went on to outline the contents of Resolution 1, which would come before convention. Described as a "firewall" resolution, its goal, according to the bishop, was to "advise the General Convention . . . of limits beyond which our diocese was unable, in all conscience, to go, in changes to Faith and Order." It amounted to a litany of complaints about various aspects of church life. It contained, for example, opposition to "liturgies that depart from the Historic Faith, especially those that use gender-neutral titles for the persons of the Holy Trinity." Putting the General Convention on notice, the resolution went on to say that it would "not accept resolutions condoning unbiblical morality." Most surprisingly, perhaps, it also declared that the Diocese of Pittsburgh would "not accept coercive canons which contradict the mind of the Anglican Communion."[16] That clause maintained that since the church "has always believed" that only men can be called to the priesthood, the canon that

15 One of the more frustrating aspects of the dispute was the bishop's insistence that we were mistaken as regard both our treatment at his hands as well as concerning the direction in which he was leading the diocese (Italics added).

16. Strictly speaking, there is no such thing as "the mind of the Anglican Communion." Historically, the churches of the Anglican Communion have followed what is affectionately known as the Lambeth Principle, in which member churches "agree to disagree"—as in the matter of women's ordination. Some opine that the Lambeth Conference's promulgations represent the mind of the Communion, but bishops alone cannot speak for the whole church. Moreover, Charles Thomas Longley, the Archbishop of Canterbury who convened the first Lambeth Conference in 1867, made it clear that Lambeth decisions are not meant to be binding on the Communion: "Such a meeting would not be competent to make declarations or lay down definitions on points of doctrine; but united worship and common counsels would greatly tend to maintain practically the unity of the faith, whilst they would bind us in straiter bonds of peace and brotherly charity" (see Lewis, *Church for the Future*, esp. ch. 1, "Whither Lambeth? Anglicanism at the Crossroads").

had recently been enacted making it illegal to withhold ordination from women should be struck down. A confusing codicil to this resolution contained the words: "While rejoicing in the gifts that ordained women have brought to this church, we also stand in solidarity with those who do not believe the Episcopal Church can make such a change to received Catholic tradition." Content aside, the resolution was presumptuous. Its proponents claimed that they witnessed "to the higher calling of the Truth as we have received it."

Despite the efforts of PEP (Progressive Episcopalians of Pittsburgh) and its ad hoc committee, TORO (Those Opposed to Resolution One), the resolution was passed overwhelmingly. It was evident to all of us that the gauntlet had been thrown down. Bishop Duncan had declared war against the Episcopal Church, and there would be no retreating. But as we came to more fully understand Duncan's "military strategy," we also were of the opinion that his theological premises were seriously flawed.

His actions made it clear to many of us that he subscribed to the "orthodox" view that members of the progressive wing of the Episcopal Church had as their goal "to create a new religion of inclusivism that stands in opposition to the biblical message of redemption."[17] Clearly even a perfunctory reading of the New Testament would show that inclusivity and redemption are not mutually exclusive. Indeed, the major acts of redemption as recorded in the New Testament, beginning with the Incarnation and continuing with the Epiphany, are in fact indicative of God's will to be inclusive, at one with humankind. The theme is given center stage in the parable of the dragnet, in which Jesus reminds us of our duty to bring into the kingdom "fish of every kind" (Matt 13:47–50). And, in reference to his crucifixion, Jesus announced his intention to "bring all people" to himself (John 12:32). The so-called orthodox movement seems to have forgotten that "catholic" means "according to the whole." While purporting to be a catholic church, it was in fact in danger of becoming a sect, dangerously

17. Virtue, "Pittsburgh Radicals Blast Orthodox Bishop."

close to establishing a religion based upon what it did *not* believe, and what it would *not* accept.

APPEAL TO THE PRIMATES

Developments during the period immediately preceding the 74th General Convention in the summer of 2003 unfolded at lightning speed. On July 15, Bishop Duncan, together with a score of his fellow bishops, sent a letter addressed to "concerned primates of the Anglican Communion," and pledged to join with them in efforts to address the current situation. The bishops who wrote the letter repudiated the leadership of the Diocese of New Westminster (Canada), which had approved rites for same-sex blessing, and declared themselves to be in impaired communion with the Anglican Church of Canada. Too, it denounced the Episcopal Church, which at the time was poised to consecrate Gene Robinson. The signatories pledged to "act in concert with" and "take counsel from" the concerned primates.[18]

I wrote to Bishop Duncan on July 21 and asked if, in light of the content of the bishops' letter to the primates, which he had signed, it was still his intention to remain in the Episcopal Church. On the following day, he wrote back, and stated: "I say it again, I am not leaving the Episcopal Church. I am the Episcopal Bishop of Pittsburgh, and so I expect to remain. Further, our Diocese is on record, by resolution of the 137th Annual Convention, as to the limits of innovation acceptable in this diocese."

---

18. Duncan et al., "Open Letter," July 15, 2003.

2

The Shot Across the Bow

IN THE SPRING OF 2003, the clergy and people of the Diocese of New Hampshire met in convention and duly elected the Rev. V. Gene Robinson, canon to the ordinary, to be their ninth bishop. Canon Robinson had a reputation as a bridge builder in the diocese, and extensive experience in Province I (the dioceses in New England) and in TEC nationally. What distinguished him from all other candidates for the office of bishop at the time, however, was that he was a partnered gay man. As Father Robinson had been elected within three months of a General Convention, the canon in force at that time required that his election be ratified by the House of Deputies and the House of Bishops, duly convened at General Convention, instead of by obtaining consent (by mail, fax, or email) from sitting bishops and standing committees. This gave more attention to the election than would have normally been the case. Hearings and debates were held; caucuses were convened; much ink was spilt; allegations were made and refuted; and orators on both sides of the issue took to their respective platforms. In the end, the election was ratified, which paved the way for the presiding bishop to take order for the consecration, which was set for November 2.

Bishop Duncan's reaction was swift and, in many ways, predictable. Following the vote in the House of Bishops, he announced that the Episcopal Church had "repudiated Holy Scripture and the historic and universal moral consensus of Christendom."[1] Almost immediately upon returning from Minneapolis, believing that the church was in "a pastoral crisis of immense proportion," he called for a special convention of the Diocese of Pittsburgh to take place at the end of September, a mere thirty days after his announcement. In a document entitled, "A Report, a Call and a Teaching for the Leadership," the bishop, stating that the General Convention, by approving both Canon Robinson's election and a plan for authorizing same-sex blessings, had "acted beyond its competence and authority to change fundamental elements of the Church's teaching." He called for the diocese to "reject these innovations and to *resist the leadership that has supported them.*" In a statement that certainly presaged imminent schism, he stated that "we have arrived at a moment within the Episcopal Church where there are actually two churches and two gospels. One church offers the fundamental good news in the values of conversion and discipleship. The other church offers its fundamental good news in the values of inclusion and liberation."

But describing the situation in this way, Bishop Duncan could justify his secession as simply implementing what had effectively already taken place, as he did later in the document when he stated: "The moment of a fundamental re-ordering of relationships within what has been the Episcopal Church and of a fundamental realignment within global Anglicanism has arrived." This would be done, declared Duncan euphemistically, by "sorting through what ecclesial structure, driven by which gospel, will gain our primary allegiance." "Sorting through," as we would learn, would take the form of changing the very structures and laws, embodied in the diocesan and national constitutions and canons, to which Duncan and the other officers of the diocese had sworn allegiance. Duncan's

---

1. All quotes in this section attributed to Bishop Duncan are taken from "A Report, a Call and a Teaching for the Leadership," issued by Bishop Duncan in September 2003 following the 74th General Convention in Minneapolis.

document, notably, also seemed to suggest that he expected some legal challenge. In it, he described the "infamous Dennis Canon," which would turn out to be a pivotal issue in our lawsuit, as an example of how "power has come to dominate Episcopal Church life over the past three decades."[2]

It is worthy of note that at the same time that Bishop Duncan announced his intention to call a special convention, he invited me to his office to ask if Calvary would be interested in directing our assessment to a source other than the diocese. He said that in light of the developments at General Convention and his reaction to it, he would understand if we felt compelled by our conscience to take such action. He added that he wanted to be on record as expressing that sentiment at the outset, so as not to put us in the role of "the bad guy." Not relishing the idea of losing an amount equal to 12 percent of the diocesan budget, however, he proffered a "Plan B," namely, that Calvary consider reducing its pledge to the diocese, a plan that would have made it possible for the diocese to receive at least a fraction of Calvary's considerable support.

DUNCAN'S "EXIT VISA": SIX RESOLUTIONS

In his announcement to the diocese, the bishop proposed that the convention pass six resolutions. As expected, those resolutions expressed disagreement with what had transpired at General Convention, but they went further than that. The resolutions laid the groundwork and the strategy for separation from the Episcopal Church, but they were phrased in such a way as to suggest that the Episcopal Church had separated itself from the Anglican Communion and from catholic Christendom.

The First Resolution declared that the actions of the convention, namely, the approval of Robinson's election and the

2. Conservatives also frequently object to the Dennis Canon because it is "new," having been passed in 1979. Would we argue, for example, that the legislation regarding women's suffrage is not binding because the Nineteenth Amendment was passed in 1919, more than a century after the First Amendment?

permitting of same-sex blessings, had the effect of removing TEC from the Anglican Communion and "rejecting its solemn responsibility to uphold and propagate the historic Faith and Order as set forth in the Book of Common Prayer." Because of these developments, according to the resolution, the General Convention decisions would not be binding on the Diocese of Pittsburgh.

Building on these premises, Resolution 2 sought, in collaboration with other "orthodox" bishops at General Convention, to call upon the primates of the Anglican Communion "for intervention in the pastoral emergency created by the apostasy of the 74th General Convention." It then went on to ask the primates of the Communion to declare, in the wake of the actions of the American Church, that the so-called orthodox bishops and their followers be "the bona fide expression of the Anglican Communion in the United States of America." This constituted a demand that the heads of the thirty-eight autonomous churches making up the Anglican Communion take action to remove the "apostate" Episcopal Church from its ranks. Moreover, such an action would declare that those who opposed General Convention's actions now constituted the faithful remnant, as it were, of American Anglicans!

The Third Resolution, by requesting that the primates provide "episcopal care for beleaguered clergy and congregations," stated, in effect, that the American House of Bishops, with the exception of those whom Bishop Duncan deemed to be "orthodox," were, by simply concurring with General Convention actions, stripped of their faculties—that is, their ability to function pastorally and sacramentally. The remedy, as perceived by the "orthodox," was to "import" bishops from overseas jurisdictions in order that they—untainted, as it were, by the actions of TEC—might minister to those now bereft of valid and bona fide episcopal leadership. Such a demand is noteworthy for at least two reasons. First, it is inconsistent with traditional church structure, since the idea that a bishop cannot function within the ecclesiastical jurisdiction of another without the approval of the local authority is an incontrovertible and sacrosanct rule in catholic Christendom, a tradition to which Duncan claimed to be loyal. Second, the demand would seek to give legitimacy to and justification for the illegal consecrations that had already taken place, which had been carried out by the Anglican Mission in America (AMiA) in Singapore and Denver, through which the breakaway Anglicans purported to provide bishops for dioceses and congregations deprived, in their opinion, of valid leadership.

In the second trio of resolutions, Bishop Duncan shifted to the more practical considerations of his proposed secession. In Resolution 4, he maintained that the actions of General Convention meant that the Episcopal Church, which depends on the financial support of parishes and dioceses for its operations, had been rendered ineligible for such support. Since such funds normally are sent by parishes to the diocesan office, which then forwards the appropriate prorated share to the national church, Bishop Duncan declared that any funds thus received would be diverted to other missionary purposes, namely to "those Anglican or Episcopal missionary agencies, dioceses and structures that serve to uphold and propagate the historic Faith and Order." In other words, the Diocese of Pittsburgh and other "orthodox" dioceses would "vote with their pocketbooks."[3]

The Fifth Resolution is like unto it, as it gives express permission to those parishes that wish to dissociate themselves from General Convention actions to redirect all or part of their diocesan assessment to missionary endeavors consonant with their theological principles. This action, it should be noted, is not an entirely new idea. As we have observed, it was at the diocesan convention of 1996 that a resolution was passed enabling congregations to redirect the "program asking" portion of their assessment to alternative organizations, and not to the coffers of the Episcopal Church

Upon reading the wording of the sixth and final resolution, it becomes apparent to the reader that Resolutions 1–5 are little more than a preamble to it. Entitled "Title to Property," it begins with a bold pronouncement that is entirely contrary to the canons.

---

3. Given Bishop Duncan's stated refusal to forward funds to the national church, those congregations in the diocese loyal to the Episcopal Church sent our funds directly to the Domestic & Foreign Missionary Society in New York.

In it, Bishop Duncan maintains that "property held by the Board of Trustees of the Church in the Episcopal Diocese of Pittsburgh for the use of a Parish, Mission Fellowship or Diocesan Organization belongs" to said entity, and that any claim to title by any other entity, notably the diocese or the Episcopal Church in the U.S., is "expressly denied." There could be no doubt that the wording of the resolution was intended to refute and contradict the wording of Title I.7.4, known as "the Dennis Canon," named for its chief author, the Rt. Rev. Walter D. Dennis, late bishop suffragan of New York, 1979–1998, and sometime chair of the Standing Committee on Constitution and Canons. Passed by the 68th General Convention in 1979, it reads as follows:

> All real and personal property held by or for the benefit of any Parish, Mission or Congregation is *held in trust for this Church* [i.e., the Episcopal Church in the United States of America] and the Diocese thereof in which such Parish, Mission or Congregation is located. (italics added)

The Dennis Canon had been written in response to a guidance from the Supreme Court of the United States that "hierarchical churches," that is, those having centralized governance, more accurately express their trust interest in all property of their denomination. It made clear that although a local congregation may hold a deed to a given property, it is in effect conditional, the condition being that the said congregation exists for the express purpose of carrying out the mission and ministry of the Episcopal Church. The canon, it should be noted, cuts both ways. Hypothetically, if a congregation decided to affiliate with the Baptist church, it would have no claim to the real property of the parish for that purpose, and the bishop would be entitled to seize the property to ensure that it remains in Episcopal hands.

A congregation, as the Dennis Canon affirms, exists in communion with the diocese and the General Convention, and is bound by both diocesan and General Convention constitution and canons. Disagreement with either "parent body" over church doctrine or polity does not give the said congregation title to the property. Legally, any officer (e.g., a diocesan bishop) of any official institution must maintain his/her fiduciary trust responsibility on behalf of the Episcopal Church. Adoption of the Dennis Canon followed the turbulent 1960s and 1970s, when parishes that were at variance with the Episcopal Church—over such issues as the ordination of women, the adoption of the 1979 *Book of Common Prayer*, and the enactment of civil rights legislation—left the Episcopal Church and attempted nevertheless to retain parish property.[4]

It is essential to emphasize at this point that the introduction of the six resolutions on the floor of the 138th Convention of the Episcopal Diocese of Pittsburgh was a serious game-changer. As I pointed out in the September 14, 2003, issue of *Agape*, the parish newsletter of Calvary Church, the issue at hand was not human sexuality:

> Let us make one thing abundantly clear. We are no longer talking about sex, sexuality or homosexuality. We are talking about the authority and governance of the church. At the General Convention, 42 diocesan bishops voted against the approval of Canon Gene Robinson's election, and yet only seven or eight of those bishops have returned to their dioceses to enact measures as Draconian as those proposed by the Bishop of Pittsburgh.[5] In other words, the overwhelming majority of bishops who disapproved of Canon Robinson's election did not deem that decision to have caused the "separating [of the Episcopal Church] from the Anglican Communion and from the One Holy Catholic and Apostolic Church."

4. So strict is the principle of property being held in trust that another section of the same canon requires a parish to seek permission of the standing committee in order to "alienate" property, e.g., to sell or donate real property to another entity.

5. Ultimately, only four dioceses went so far as to purport to withdraw from TEC: Pittsburgh, Quincy (IL), Fort Worth, and San Joaquin; although it should be noted that the Diocese of South Carolina took similar action in 2012 following the deposition of its bishop, Mark Lawrence.

Although the official separation of Duncan and his followers from the Diocese of Pittsburgh and the inauguration of the Anglican Church in North America did not take place until 2008, the "shot across the bow" was unquestionably fired during the diocesan convention five years earlier. By using the actions of the 2003 General Convention as a claimed basis, and maintaining that they created "a conflict into which the decisions of others have now plunged us," Robert Duncan appeared to a number of us to be leading members of the Diocese of Pittsburgh down the path of separation from the Episcopal Church. It is for this reason that the clergy, wardens, and vestry of Calvary Episcopal Church decided to file suit against Robert William Duncan et al. in the Allegheny County Court of Common Pleas. It is imperative to understand that our action was taken neither to champion gay rights nor to uphold the validity of Gene Robinson's consecration. Indeed, the vestry was not of a single mind as to either. The action was taken for two purposes: first, to uphold the rule of law, both civil and ecclesiastical; and second, to maintain the integrity and to preserve the assets of the Diocese of Pittsburgh of the Episcopal Church in the United States of America.

It should be pointed out, however, that prior to taking legal actions we communicated our concern about the special convention and the proposed resolutions in a letter to Bishop Duncan on September 17, 2003. In it the following points were made, which formed the basis of our argument in the lawsuit:

1. The content of the resolutions suggests that they are intended to achieve a separation from the Episcopal Church in the United States of America.

2. The resolutions seek to render null and void certain acts of the 74th General Convention, and to authorize actions, including expenditure of funds, contrary to the purposes of the Episcopal Church.

3. The resolutions appear to attempt to alter the title and/or use of property from the title and use provided under the statues of the Commonwealth of Pennsylvania and the operative

legal documents. These resolutions appear to be a precursor to the potential transfer of property outside of the Episcopal Church in the United States of America and/or the Episcopal Diocese of Pittsburgh.

Calvary was not alone in its efforts to attempt to stay the bishop from his intended course of action. The Rev. Robert Banse, for example, then rector of St.

Paul's Church, Mount Lebanon, a parish that saw itself as "divided" and which "pledged to serve as a bridge over the chasm that exists" in the Episcopal Church, stated that the separation that the bishop advocated was contrary to both the spirit of the New Testament and the spirit of Anglicanism, a separation that he further described as one with "grave ecclesiastical and legal implications."[6]

6. Banse, open letter to Duncan, September 14, 2003.

3

Primatial Promulgations

The "recent unpleasantness," it can be observed, proved to be instructive, inasmuch as it provided, if unwittingly, a kind of crash course in Anglican polity. Episcopalians could no longer be complacent in the insularity of their parish churches. They were suddenly aware that they belonged to a worldwide family, which, like other families, had its share of dysfunction. A meeting of the primates of the Anglican Communion, which previously might not have been a very newsworthy item for Episcopalians, was catapulted into the category of banner headlines. In October 2003, Rowan Williams, who had recently succeeded George Carey as Archbishop of Canterbury, having attended his first meeting of the primates in Brazil only five months before, summoned his archiepiscopal brethren to Lambeth Palace in London to discuss the ramifications for the Communion of two recent bombshell events on the other side of the Atlantic, namely, the approval of a rite for same-sex blessings in the Diocese of New Westminster (Canada), and the approval of the election of V. Gene Robinson, a partnered gay priest, as bishop of New Hampshire.

The primates' statement issued at the close of that gathering was characterized by a conciliatory and irenic tone, and reflected their commitment, as expressed at Lambeth 1988, that "authority in the Church works *through* rather than in spite of disagreement." Nevertheless, the document allowed that Robinson's consecration could bring the Anglican Communion to "a crucial and critical point" and that it could in fact be "put in jeopardy," especially if provinces declared themselves to be "out of communion" with TEC.[1]

Since the primates' statement dealt primarily with the theological issues engendered by recent synodical actions on the part of Canada and the United States, it had little direct reference to our lawsuit. But its pronouncements did much to describe the climate in which our canonical problems would be thrashed out. The primates, for example, addressed the "question of the parity of our own canon law," and acknowledged "a legitimate diversity of interpretation that arises in the church," pointing out, however, that such diversity "does not mean that some of us take the authority of Scripture more lightly than others." Of especial significance was the provision made for "episcopal visitors," bishops who would minister to disaffected Anglicans in a given province, "*whose role is duly authorized within the province and/or diocese in which they are to function.*" Such a practice would adhere to the time-honored prohibition of parallel jurisdictions as iterated at successive Lambeth Conferences, and differs, therefore, from the recommendation on the part of secessionists in some provinces for unauthorized alternative episcopal oversight.

In this regard, the primates' statement reminded the Communion of the resolutions passed by the bishops at the 1998 Lambeth Conference, especially Resolution I.10. But notably, instead of emphasizing the part of the resolution that rejected homosexual practice as being "incompatible with Scripture," it held up the part of that resolution that is often overlooked: "to listen to the experience of homosexual persons . . . and to recognize that baptized, believing and faithful persons, regardless of sexual orientation, are full members of the Body of Christ," and that there is "a need for ongoing study on questions of human sexuality." But the most

1. All quotes in this chapter are from the "Statement by the Primates" issued October 16, 2003.

significant primatial decision was a request to the Archbishop of Canterbury to make every effort to put flesh and bones on another Lambeth 1998 resolution, namely the creation of a commission that would consider "maintaining communion within and between provinces when grave difficulties arise." Given the fact that such grave difficulties had already arisen, the document urged that the commission should produce an initial report within twelve months. That body would become known as the Lambeth Commission on Communion, commonly called the "Eames Commission,"[2] and its seminal document, the Windsor Report.[3]

2. The commission was named for its chair, the Most Rev. Dr. Robin Eames, Archbishop of Armagh and Primate of All Ireland, 1986–2006. He had previously served as chair of the Archbishop of Canterbury's Commission on Women in the Episcopate (1988–89) and chair of the Inter-Anglican Theological and Doctrinal Commission (1991).

3. As the Windsor Report was released in October 2004, we shall address its significance later.

4

The Die Is Cast

ON OCTOBER 24, 2003, a complaint in equity was filed in the Allegheny County Court of Common Pleas by Calvary Episcopal Church, the rector, the Rev. Dr. Harold T. Lewis, and senior warden, Philip Richard Roberts. We were later joined in the action by St. Stephen's Church, Wilkinsburg, and its rector, the Rev. Diane Shepard. St. Stephen's, a parish founded by Calvary in 1878, has long been considered one of the "progressive" congregations of the diocese, and therefore a predictable ally.

It is noteworthy, therefore, that the suit was later joined by Herman S. ("Bud") Harvey, an attorney and a member of St. Stephen's, Sewickley, a large, staunchly conservative parish that had long been supportive of Bishop Duncan's initiatives. A former warden of St. Stephen's, Mr. Harvey petitioned to intervene in our suit to assure that the property utilized by St. Stephen's, Sewickley, would remain a part of, and would be held in trust for, the Episcopal Church and the Episcopal Diocese of Pittsburgh, and not be used for any purpose inconsistent with the interests of the Episcopal Church. In his petition, he set forth provisions of the deed to the property upon which St. Stephen's sits, executed in May 1864, when the parish was incorporated, which specified the use to be made of the property, viz., that it "be held in trust for the sole use and benefit of the association of the Protestant Episcopal Church at the Borough of Sewickley." It would be helpful, we think, to cite the wording of St. Stephen's "Articles of Incorporation," which were still in effect at the time of the filing of the lawsuit, as it lays out the understanding of property ownership as understood by the Episcopal Church, and its relationship to adherence to church teachings, an understanding that formed the basis of the Dennis Canon passed by the General Convention more than a century later:

> This congregation acknowledges itself to be a member of and belong to the Diocese of Pittsburgh in the Commonwealth of Pennsylvania and the Protestant Episcopal Church in the United States of America. As such it expressly adopts and recognizes the authority of the Constitution and Canons, doctrines, disciplines and worship of the Protestant Episcopal Church in the United States of America.

A complaint in equity is in effect a demand for fairness, a plea for justice. Calvary Church believed that the resolutions passed at the special convention were inconsistent with the legal document governing the diocese. The complaint was filed not against the diocese, as is commonly believed, but against the bishop and assistant bishop of Pittsburgh, certain members of the board of trustees of the diocese,[1] and certain members of the standing committee of the diocese,[2] as diocesan officers, to prevent them from transferring ownership of any church property. Calvary, it must be pointed out, filed suit not only on its own behalf, but also in its asserted capacity as a trustee *ad litem* for the Diocese of Pittsburgh.

---

1. The board of trustees is a group of laypersons—some elected, others appointed—charged with the responsibility of administering the fiscal affairs of the diocese.

2. The standing committee consists of four clergy and four laypersons, all elected by diocesan convention, who act as a council of advice to the bishop. The committee also has certain other canonical responsibilities, including approving candidates for ordination, and consenting, on behalf of the diocese, to the election of bishops. When the see is "vacant," i.e., when there is no bishop, the standing committee is the ecclesiastical authority (although this rule varies from diocese to diocese).

Such a procedure allows members of an unincorporated association—in this case, the Diocese of Pittsburgh—to assert the need for compliance with the association's constitution and bylaws. In other words, Calvary, a founding parish of and major contributor to the diocese[3] since the latter's founding in 1865,[4] asserted that it was suing on behalf of all the members of the diocese. Its premise was simple: it was based on the principle, held both by the Episcopal Church and in American jurisprudence, that the members of an organization are bound by the previously agreed upon rules of that organization, in this case, the constitutions and canons of the Episcopal Church and the diocese, which had been acceded to, recognized, and adopted by the diocese. Although the court did not formally grant Calvary *ad litem* status, the stipulation approved by the court that resolved the suit, as we shall see later, achieved benefits for all loyal Episcopalians in the diocese.

The suit maintained that no one can hold office in that organization and at the same time, among other things, disregard its rules. In the words of the complaint, Duncan and others, "in disregard of the Constitution and Canons that granted them authority over such property and assets," have "failed to discharge their obligations" because they have "threatened improperly to transfer, and/or have transferred, property contrary to such interests," namely, those of the Episcopal Church, the diocese, and Calvary Church and its congregation.

An Associated Press article quoted me as saying that the lawsuit had nothing to do with Gene Robinson or homosexuality, but is about the Episcopal Church. The article went on to report that I also commented that "the Court will uphold our position because the people of the Episcopal Church in this diocese are entitled to the use and the enjoyment of their property." Bishop Duncan, calling the lawsuit a "power play" and insisting that it

3. At the time of the filing of the lawsuit, when there were approximately seventy-five congregations in the diocese, Calvary's contribution to the diocese, an "assessment" predicated on the size of its membership and income, amounted to approximately 12 percent of the diocesan budget.

4. Calvary was founded in 1855, and at that time was part of the Diocese of Pennsylvania, which was made up of the entire Commonwealth.

was connected to the Episcopal Church's decision to consecrate a gay man, remarked, "I think the action on their part is definitely premature, since what we've done is try to protect all the church's property."[5] The lawsuit, not surprisingly, was widely reported in both the church and secular press. Dr. J. Robert Wright, a professor at General Theological Seminary and historiographer of the Episcopal Church, predicted that the suit "could be a prototype of efforts to keep church property intact in the aftermath of a split in the denomination." The London *Times*, which described Calvary as "a well-heeled congregation of doctors and lawyers," and "a flagship of liberal Episcopalians," referred to our suit as "the first volley in the much-feared legal battle over church property that could result from a schism in the worldwide Anglican Communion."[6]

5. "Episcopal Priest Files Suit over Property," October 26, 2003.
6. Bone, "Church Begins Property Wrangle," October 27, 2003.

5

The "Other Convention"

WHEN ON FRIDAY, NOVEMBER 7, 2003 Robert William Duncan rapped his gavel to declare that the 138th Convention of the Diocese of Pittsburgh was called to order, there was a palpable tension in the air, a tension doubtless without precedent in the history of the diocese. The clerical and lay deputies were still reeling from the impact of the resolutions passed at the special convention that took place six weeks earlier, which presaged a separation between at least some persons in the diocese and the Episcopal Church. The bishops and trustees and members of the standing committee of the diocese had been sued in civil court within the past fortnight by one of the parishes in their diocese, regarding the issues arising from that potential separation. Moreover, the main order of business of the convention was the "first reading" of Resolution 1, a proposed amendment to Article I, Section 1, of the Constitution of the Diocese.[1] Building on themes already expressed at the special convention, it read:

1. Constitutional and canonical changes require approval at two successive conventions. It should also be noted that in Resolution 2 another article of the Constitution came before the convention: Article 3, Section 2, on canonical residence of clergy. By striking the word "actually" from the article, it made it possible for clergy living outside the geographical boundaries of the diocese to enjoy the rights and privileges of canonical membership, especially voice,

> In cases where the provisions of the Constitution and
> Canons of the Church in the Diocese of Pittsburgh speak
> to the contrary, or where Resolutions of the Conventions
> of the said Diocese have determined the Constitution
> and Canons of the Protestant Episcopal Church in the
> United States of America, or resolutions of its General
> Convention, to be contrary to the historic Faith and Or-
> der of the one holy catholic and apostolic church, the
> local determination shall prevail.

By declaring that resolutions passed and canons enacted locally trumped any decision (by canon or resolution) of the national General Convention, the proposed resolution was a de facto declaration of separation from the national church. The proposers, however, did not see it in this way. David Brannen, who moved the resolution, declared the change necessary "for the sake of conscience [and] to protect ourselves from any attempt to be co-opted or coerced into compliance with teaching or practices which we believe are morally unacceptable or constitutionally illegal." The Rev. Geoff Chapman, rector of St. Stephen's, Sewickley, referred to the amendment as a "fundamental safeguard of organizational health."

The Rev. Diane Shepard, rector of St. Stephen's, Wilkinsburg, appealed the ruling of the chair that the motion was in order, and pointed out that even if passed, "this motion is out of order and will be null and void" since "it is a fundamental principle of any parliamentary assembly that any motion that violates the bylaws or constitution of the organization is out of order." The Rev. Bruce Robison, rector of St. Andrew's, Highland Park, reminded the

---

seat, and vote at diocesan convention. On the one hand, this change was in conformity with the practice of other dioceses, who recognize as canonically resident clergy who, for example, began their ministry in the diocese and then went on to teach at a seminary outside the diocese, or to do missionary work in some other part of the Anglican Communion. The problem is that the change in this instance contemplated the ability of clergy who are canonically resident elsewhere but who are sympathetic to the ideological and theological positions of the Diocese of Pittsburgh, to *become* members of the Diocese of Pittsburgh. Resolution 2 was significant because it speaks to what might be called Bishop Duncan's missionary strategy.

convention of the constitutional phrase "unqualified accession," which describes the nature of the relationship between dioceses and the constitution and canons of the national church. When Bishop Duncan refuted Father Robison's interpretation by stating that "this diocese was not part of the accession," Joan Gundersen, a noted church historian from Redeemer, Squirrel Hill, produced the document from the national archive, which attested that the Diocese of Pittsburgh gave such unqualified accession when it was founded in 1865.

Robert Devlin, chancellor of the diocese,[2] responded to Dr. Gundersen's remarks by ruling that the article does not state that diocesan constitution and canons cannot be subsequently changed. Moreover, denying the fact that the Episcopal Church is a hierarchical one (under which system a diocese is answerable to authorities outside itself, unlike so-called standalone churches—a key argument in our lawsuit) he put forward the novel argument that TEC is a confederation, in effect a group of autonomous bodies who can make up their own rules as they go along, adding that the extant article "does not say that we are required to concede all rights to the national church." When Richard Spagnolli from St. Stepehen's, Wilkinsburg, pressed Chancellor Devlin to rule on whether the passing of the resolution was tantamount to a rejection of the constitution of the national church, the bishop prevented him from answering by stating that time for debate had expired.

Because of the potential ramifications of the vote on Resolution 1, and because delegates to the 138th Convention would be called upon to decide, in effect, if it is their desire to function as part of the Episcopal Church, it was strongly felt by many that there should be a roll call vote, so that there would be a record of each delegate's position. Moreover, as some delegates observed, those voting in favor of such a resolution might subject themselves to presentment, i.e., former canonical charges against them, possibly

2. The chancellor is the bishop's legal counsel. Mr. Devlin was one of a team of chancellors recently appointed to the bishop. The former chancellor, Charles B. Jarrett of Calvary Church, who had served continuously since the episcopate of Robert Appleyard, did not interpret the canons in such a way that would be consonant with the theological views of Bishop Duncan.

for abandoning the ministry of the church. Perhaps for that reason, many of those clergy voting in favor of the resolution, not wanting to be identified or singled out, were not in favor of a roll call vote. Accordingly, the Rev. Patrick Dominguez of St. Stephen's, Sewickley, moved to suspend the rules of convention as they relate to a roll call vote. The bishop overruled objections to this motion, declared that the matter of suspension of rules of order is not debatable, and called for a vote of "ayes" and "nays." At the end of the day, the resolution was passed by a voice vote.

In commenting on the state of affairs after the 138th Convention, Bishop Duncan observed that, inasmuch as nothing become official until the ratifications of such actions at the 139th Convention a year later, "nothing has changed." I believe that nothing could be farther from the truth. The situation into which the diocese was thrust was in many ways akin to a married couple who have decided to divorce, but who for a variety of reasons still find themselves under the same roof. In fact, the diocesan situation was far worse, for whereas the couple may, in this admittedly awkward period, learn that there was still a modicum of affection between them even though their marriage had come to an end, there was no such feeling abroad in the Diocese of Pittsburgh, in which the conservative faction saw themselves as the wronged party in the relationship, the progressive element, in their opinion, having caused by their actions the unhappy divisions in which we all found ourselves.

There had been, for some time, a "great gulf fixed" between the two groups, which was neither bridged nor narrowed by the bishop's actions and rhetoric. The actions of the 2003 diocesan convention made it impossible for that chasm ever to be crossed again. I expressed my opinion of this situation on the floor of convention, pointing out to the bishop:

> You have assured us that you are not leaving the Episcopal Church, yet you endorse resolutions which belie that promise. You have asserted that we are one church of miraculous expectations, yet you have publicly declared that we have become two churches preaching two

irreconcilable gospels. You have purported that we are a church of missionary grace, yet the budget approved yesterday makes no provision to support our parent body, the Domestic and Foreign Missionary Society. You have asked us to work together in areas that we can, yet having deemed many of us to be unorthodox, apostate or schismatic, you have rendered such collaboration an impossibility.

The decisions of the 138th Convention made it a certainty that no further pronouncements encouraging unity of purpose among those in the diocesan family would be forthcoming. It was clear that the majority of the clergy and people of the diocese had set their face toward Buenos Aires. But we took no small comfort in the hope that, because of our legal actions, the "merger" with the Southern Cone could not be financed, in whole or in part, by funds belonging to the Episcopal Diocese of Pittsburgh.

6

Battle Lines Are Drawn
The Chapman Memo

SCANT WEEKS AFTER THE adjournment of the convention, the heretofore clandestine master plan of the separatists saw the light of day. The *Washington Post*, on January 14, 2004, published an article entitled, "Plan to Supplant Episcopal Church USA Is Revealed."[1] The article contained the report of a memorandum written by the Rev. Geoff Chapman, rector of St. Stephen's Church, Sewickley, and arguably Bishop Duncan's most loyal lieutenant and supporter. Disseminated on December 28, 2003, it was intended to be confidential, its author urging his readers to share it "in hard copy only with people you fully trust," and not to pass it on electronically to anyone under any circumstances! Nevertheless, the veil of secrecy was lifted within two weeks.

Chapman wrote the memo "on behalf of the American Anglican Council (AAC) and their Bishops' Committee on Adequate Episcopal Oversight" (AEO), whose members envisioned a plan that would provide for the ministrations of "orthodox" bishops for those Episcopalians who believed that the 2003 General Convention resulted in "the rejection of the historic faith and the rejection

1. Cooperman, "Plan to Supplant."

of biblical and Communion authority." The AAC, as the *Post* article described it, was "a Washington-based group marshaling opposition to the Nov. 2 consecration of New Hampshire Bishop V. Gene Robinson." But AEO was seen merely as a stopgap measure. Ultimately, Chapman explained, the network of parishes under the AAC umbrella (whose members would eventually ally themselves with the Anglican Network) could constitute a "replacement jurisdiction," that is, it could supplant the Episcopal Church as the legitimate American branch of the Anglican Communion.

This was not a new concept for Chapman. As early as 1999, representing an organization known as First Promise,[2] he and several other American conservative leaders met with a group of Anglican primates in Uganda, and broached the idea of submitting U.S. churches to Anglican control:

> We believe that it is essential that much of the Episcopal Church be rebuked by the international communion and called to repentance. We ask for a new jurisdiction on American soil, under the temporary oversight of an overseas province . . . Such a jurisdiction would also provide a visible restraint and warning to those who oppose the Gospel.[3]

And lest the recipients of the memo think that the plan outlined was meant to be merely a spiritual or ideological exercise,

2. First Promise, a precursor to AMiA, was an organization of conservative clergy that came into being shortly after the 1997 General Convention. Its name derives from its belief that "when the church itself departs from the faith it has received, the loyalty of faithful Christians must be to apostolic faith rather than the authority of canons, institutions and bishops." They further stated that they would not be bound "in the exercise of our priestly ministries, by the legal or geographical boundaries of any parish or diocese" (*United Voice*, cited in Kirkpatrick, *Episcopal Church in Crisis*, 10).

3. Geoffrey Chapman, "Presentation to the Kampala Meeting Held by Association of Anglican Congregations on Mission (AACOM)" (1999), cited in Hassett, *Anglican Communion in Crisis*, 103. Such statements reveal that the idea of "realignment" with an overseas jurisdiction and submitting to its authority, among the actions challenged in the Calvary lawsuit, were strategies conceived long before a similar plan was adopted, allegedly in response to the election and consecration of Gene Robinson in 2003.

Chapman added, "We seek to retain ownership of our property as we move into this realignment." This statement caused Jim Solheim, then director of the Episcopal News Service, to comment that this strategy "is going to plunge us into litigation for decades."Chapman's document did not want for specificity. It indicated that member congregations should form "clusters" of parishes so that they would be a stronger force to be reckoned with, pointing out that "any isolated parish that moves alone into the revisionist line of fire . . . is going to be in peril." It encouraged them, too, to "creatively direct finances" and to participate in "a faithful disobedience of canon law on a widespread basis." The most egregious example of such disobedience, reflective of Bishop Duncan's new theology of *episcope*, was to "seek transfer of parish oversight across geographic diocesan boundaries." In a section entitled "Be careful of your language," Chapman warned: "Don't declare yourself 'out of communion' with your diocesan bishops as such statements have been used as evidence for canonical action against clergy ('abandonment of communion')." He recommended instead the use of such phrases as "impaired" or "damaged."[4]

The Chapman memo played an important role in clarifying the nature of the ongoing dispute between the Episcopal Church and those who sought to replace it. In the first place, it was the first admission of a plan of secession after a series of denials on the part of the AAC, which had maintained that their desire was not to leave the Episcopal Church but to work within it to effect change in its canonical structure (a line of argument often used by Bishop Duncan). Moreover, the memo offered the playbook that would be followed to achieve that end, including the role to be played by foreign bishops, especially Global South primates.[5] Even more

---

4. Ibid.

5. The Global South is comprised of most of the Third World provinces of the Anglican Communion, found in Africa and Asia. They are noted, with few exceptions, for their evangelical churchmanship and their conservative theology, especially regarding matters of sexual ethics. Its name is a reminder that the numerical strength of Anglicanism is in the Southern Hemisphere, once a fertile mission field, and no longer in the Northern Hemisphere, from which missionaries were sent.

significantly, the memo's bold statements about the intention of the separatists to redirect funds and to claim title to church property were a direct challenge to the Dennis Canon. In the words of an article that appeared in *The Witness*, a progressive journal, "The Chapman letter reveals the AAC's 'realignment' for what it really is—the overthrow of the Episcopal Church by extra-legal means."[6]

Another progressive blogger put it this way:

> The letter speaks for itself. Property, not piety is keeping dissident parishes in the Episcopal Church. In the longer term, the AAC expects to use foreign intervention to trump American law and the Episcopal Church Constitution and Canons. Its leaders are assuring dissident parishes that the Anglican primates, a consultative body with no governing authority or standing in the United States, will ride to the rescue of network parishes, negotiate property settlements and transfer the assets of a 2.3 million-member church to a group representing perhaps a tenth of that body.[7]

6. "Groups Call for Repudiation," January 20, 2004.

7. Father Jake, "For Those Who Missed It," March 30, 2007.

7

An Attempt to Put the Anglican House in Order

The Windsor Report

"DECENTLY AND IN ORDER" is a biblical phrase (1 Cor 14:40) that has long resonated with Anglicans. It is an expression most often invoked in reference to the liturgy, in its rubrical correctness, as set out in the *Book of Common Prayer* and a host of worship manuals, which instruct us regarding how and when to kneel, stand, sit, walk, pray, sing, and speak. Anglicans would be surprised to learn, therefore, that Paul gives this advice to the faithful at Corinth not in relation to their worship, but as regards their ministry of prophecy. "So my brethren," he writes, "desire to prophesy, and do not forbid speaking in tongues; but all things should be done decently and in order" (1 Cor 14:39–40).

By all accounts, the Anglican Communion has been in disarray. (Indeed, given the circumstances of its founding, it can be argued that it has always been. The late bishop and professor Stephen Sykes has even described the Communion as "messy."[1]) No longer do people believe that the Communion is held together by

1. Sykes et al., eds., *Study of Anglicanism.*

the Prayer Book. English is no longer the predominant tongue of its members, most of whom are people of color from the Third World. The American Prayer Book declares that the ministers of the church are "laypersons, bishops, priests and deacons"—in that order! The ordained ministries of women have been accepted, indeed embraced, in most of the provinces of the Communion. As colonial structures crumble, the Church and the nations in which she finds herself have raised up indigenous leadership. As various communities of the marginalized claim their place at the table, such bodies as the General Convention of TEC and the Lambeth Conference have declared that homosexual persons are children of God entitled to the ministrations of the church. Their desire to be ordained and to enter into lifelong committed relationships has been met with staunch resistance on the one hand and fervent advocacy on the other. This is not a new phenomenon. Change in the church has never been readily accepted. Charles Hefling observes:

> There has seldom been a time when Christians were not embroiled in one noisy dispute or another, and unedifying though the quarrels were, their result in the long run have been to refine and clarify what Christianity is and what it is for. If, as the adage says, the church is always getting reformed, its reformation seems to go hand in hand with controversy.[2]

In every age, prophets have arisen interpreting the signs of the times for the people of God, declaring the acceptable year of the Lord's favor for his people; and in every age, such utterances have led to the desire to tidy things up by interpreting, correcting, challenging (and sometimes muting) the prophets, and establishing redefined and acceptable boundaries within which the church as a community of faith can operate.

At the beginning of the third millennium, the Windsor Report functioned in this capacity for the Anglican Communion. In the foreword to that document, Archbishop Eames, citing the "major divisions" caused by the actions of the 74th General Convention

---

2. Hefling, *Our Selves, Our Souls, and Bodies*, Introduction.

of the Episcopal Church, the Diocese of New Westminster, as well as the growing practice under which bishops from some provinces have performed episcopal acts in other dioceses or provinces without the consent or approval of the incumbent bishop, wrote:

> The Lambeth Commission was established in October 2003 by the Archbishop of Canterbury at the request of the Anglican Primates. The mandate spoke of the problems being experienced as a consequence of the above developments and the need to seek a way forward which would encourage communion within the Anglican Communion. It did not demand judgment by the Commission on sexuality issues. Rather it requested consideration of ways in which communion and understanding could be enhanced where serious differences threatened the life of a diverse worldwide Church. In short, how does the Anglican Communion address relationships between its component parts in a true spirit of communion?[3]

The report, although occasioned for the most part by matters having to do with human sexuality, was virtually silent on the question of the morality of homosexual acts or same-sex unions. It would appear that it accepted as given that the issues raised would continue to be present in the life of the Church, and therefore it was primarily concerned with how the Church could somehow learn to live with differences of theology, behavior, and practice. The report, it can be said, was concerned with preserving a sense of unity among the members of the Anglican family, however fragile, and therefore focused exclusively on actions that might impair that unity.[4]

As regards the relationship between the Communion and TEC, the report was not nearly as castigatory as many had feared (or hoped). In his pre-convention address, Bishop Duncan had stated that, according to a report leaked in the London press, the Windsor Report would recommend that TEC be excluded from the Anglican Communion. In point of fact, the Eames Commission

---

3. Lambeth Commission on Communion, "Windsor Report," 5.

4. See Kirkpatrick, *Episcopal Church in Crisis*, 68ff.

recommended the following, using language that stopped well short of making demands of the American Episcopal Church:

- [TEC] be *invited to express its regret* that the proper constraints of the bonds of affection were breached . . . and that such an expression of regret would represent the desire of [TEC] to remain within the Communion;

- . . . those who took part as consecrators of Gene Robinson should be *invited to consider* whether they should withdraw themselves from representative functions in the Anglican Communion . . . ;

- [TEC] be *invited to effect a moratorium* on the election and consent to the consecration of any candidate to the episcopate who is living in a same gender union until some new consensus in the Anglican Communion emerges;

- . . . the Instruments of Unity, through the Joint Standing Committee, find practical ways in which the listening process commended by the Lambeth Conference in 1998 may be taken forward . . . on the underlying issue of same gender relationships.[5]

The report also made provision for "caring for all the churches" through delegated episcopal pastoral oversight (DEPO) as proposed by the House of Bishops of TEC, as opposed to the establishment of parallel jurisdictions favored by the conservatives. Those bishops who have refused to utilize DEPO were urged to "reconsider" their positions.

The final section of the report seemed far more ominous. It provided for the "very real danger that we will not choose to walk together."[6] Possible options in such an instance included mediation and arbitration; non-invitation to relevant representative bodies and meetings; imposition of observer status at such meetings; and

---

5. Lambeth Commission on Communion, "Windsor Report," 53–54.
6. Ibid., 60.

as an absolute last resort, withdrawal from membership in the Communion.

Neither conservatives nor progressives in TEC were especially pleased with the Windsor Report. Most conservative leaders were disappointed in the tone of the report, lamenting the fact that it had no "teeth," and therefore could not really insist on compliance. David Anderson, president of the American Anglican Council, for example, predicted that liberal bishops would not respect the request for a moratorium, and that they would respond to the request for apology with mere token gestures. In addition, the report did not establish a strict delineation between those who are bona fide Anglicans and those who are not. Duncan dismissed the Windsor Report: "It's more about family than it is about faith, and more concerned about unity than it is about truth."[7]

The progressive camp, for its part, took umbrage with the report on several fronts. Among the most salient of these was the report's contention that both TEC and New Westminster had failed to make a "serious attempt to offer an explanation to, or consult meaningfully with the Communion as a whole about the significant development of theology which alone could justify the recent moves."[8] Presiding Bishop Frank Griswold took exception to this allegation, stating that for at least thirty years, TEC had been listening to the experiences and reflecting on the witness of gays and lesbians in our congregations.[9] Liberal church folk also reacted negatively to the report's suggestions that the American and Canadian provinces had exercised their autonomy inappropriately, and had not consulted with the Instruments of Unity. I would suggest that such thinking did not sit well with progressive thinkers, among those, Episcopalians who see the issue of homosexuality as not only a theological issue but a justice issue. Waiting for (the predictably unlikely) Communion-wide acceptance would be seen as

7. See LeBlanc, "Windsor Report."

8. Lambeth Commission on Communion, "Windsor Report," 20.

9. Pew Research Center, "Anglicanism and Global Affairs," October 19, 2004.

being as effective as having waited to the U.S. government's blanket approval of civil rights.

Some view the Windsor Report as a noble attempt to appease the polarities of Anglicanism. For example, it gave lip service to the idea that the eternal truth of the gospel should lead the church "to an appreciation of diversity within the life of the church . . . to be welcomed as normal and healthy."[10] But, as Kirkpatrick observes, "when diversity ought to trump uniformity and when the maintenance of the Communion trumps diversity is never made entirely clear."[11]

But the fact that the Communion did not implode, and the fact that there was not a widespread demand to withhold invitations from American and Canadian bishops from the Lambeth Conference scheduled to take place four years later, speaks, perhaps, to the real success of the Windsor Report. It managed to appeal to the long cherished idea of "bonds of affection" to keep the Anglican family together. What was accomplished on behalf of thirty-eight provinces of Anglicanism was, unfortunately, not achievable in the eleven counties in southwestern Pennsylvania known as the Episcopal Diocese of Pittsburgh.

10. Lambeth Commission on Communion, "Windsor Report," 37.
11. Kirkpatrick, *Episcopal Church in Crisis*, 72.

8

"Curiouser and Curiouser"
The 2004 Diocesan Convention

THE INK WAS NOT dry on the Windsor Report when the 139th Convention of the Diocese of Pittsburgh was called to order at St. Philip's, Moon Township, in November 2004. It is reasonable to assume that the bishop of Pittsburgh, disappointed as he was with the report, might have felt robbed of some of his thunder. The agenda of the convention suggested that Duncan would have welcomed the opportunity to announce that the Episcopal Church had been removed from the Anglican Communion. But the major task of the convention was to ratify decisions made at the previous convention concerning the proposed separation of the diocese from TEC. A series of specific resolutions was introduced to achieve that end. From a logical point of view, the diocese had to first declare independence from TEC. This was done through the passage of a resolution that affirmed that the diocese is no longer bound by the constitution and canons of TEC or the resolutions of its General Convention, in those cases in which the diocese deemed such resolutions to be "contrary to the historic Faith and Order of the one holy catholic and apostolic church." Its decision not to be bound by the policies of TEC led to the conclusion that the diocese should not lend its financial support to the national church body. This was accomplished by removing "national Church" as a line item in the diocesan budget.

It is noteworthy that the resolutions that were enacted took place under the watchful eye of the Most Rev. Henry Luke Orombi, archbishop of Uganda, one of the Global South primates, whose province was also a member of the Anglican Communion Network. He was in attendance as "chaplain" to the convention. His presence was an outward and visible sign of the diocese's connection to those churches with which Bishop Duncan and his "orthodox" counterparts enjoyed a special relationship. Indeed, Orombi had declared that the only American Anglicans with whom his province was in communion were those who were members of the Anglican Communion Network.[1] The archbishop's presence, therefore, was a sign that the departure of the bishop of the Diocese of Pittsburgh and his followers from the Episcopal Church was imminent. Indeed, such close affiliations caused many in the diocese to believe that when "realignment" took place, it might be with one of the African provinces with which Pittsburgh was closely allied, such as Uganda, Nigeria, or Rwanda.

This brings us to another factor in the development of conservative Anglicanism in America that is often overlooked. It is no coincidence that the church groups who make up membership in the secessionist movements are almost entirely white. Even prior to the debate on homosexuality, some conservative groupings of Episcopalians began to break away in response to the progressive nature of TEC, which aligned itself with the civil rights movement. One such group is the Anglican Province of America, whose website states, "In the 1960s, the Episcopal Church in the United States (ECUSA) increasingly involved itself with the Civil Rights Movement. Some in the church began to question areas of ECUSA's involvement which seemed to them to be supporting

1. According to Hassett, to Anglican leaders like Orombi "shared Anglican identity is defined through mutual recognition, rather than membership in the worldwide Anglican polity . . . in which the Episcopal Church remains the only official Anglican body in the United States" (*Anglican Communion in Crisis*, 153).

radical causes."[2] It goes on to say that it was felt that a new body was needed in order to preserve traditional Anglicanism. Such instances point to the reality that the separatist movement did not come into being in response to the election and consecration of Gene Robinson. Episcopalians unhappy with such developments as Prayer Book revision, women's ordination, and the church's involvement in civil rights, as well as its position on gays in the ministry, all helped to lay the groundwork for secession.

In this connection, many have opined that a predominant factor in the conservative movement in TEC has been the loss of white male hegemony. Ian Douglas, for example, the bishop of Connecticut and formerly professor at the Episcopal Divinity School and a member of the Anglican Consultative Council, observed:

> The radical transition afoot in the Anglican Communion is terrifying, for it means that Anglicans in the West—especially heterosexual, white, male clerics—will no longer have the power and control that they have enjoyed for so long. They thus are anxious, confused, lost in a sea of change. The movement from being a colonial and modern church to that of a postcolonial and postmodern community in Christ, with its concomitant specter of loss, is vigorously countered by those who have been historically the most privileged in the Communion. Various attempts to reassert control, reassert power, put Humpty Dumpty back together again, with all the King's horses and all the King's men, are dominating inter-Anglican conversations at this point in history.[3]

As we return to our discussion of the actions at the Pittsburgh diocesan convention, we see other attempts to reassert power. To underscore its contempt for the national Church, a resolution supporting the work of Episcopal Relief and Development (formerly the Presiding Bishop's Fund for World Relief) was tabled indefinitely. This was not surprising since Bishop Duncan had already

2. Wikipedia, "Anglican Province of America."
3. Douglas, "Exigency of Times and Occasions," 31.

launched the rival Anglican Relief and Development to provide an avenue for the primate of Uganda and others to receive funding from American sources outside of TEC's structure. As one delegate opined, "When I give a dollar, I want the name of Jesus to travel on that dollar until it arrives at its destination. If you give to the national church, the name of Jesus does not travel with that dollar!" A resolution supporting women priests was also tabled, as delegates, including several women priests, argued that passage of the resolution would be offensive to those (e.g., many in the Anglican Network) who oppose women's ordination.[4]

"VOTE THEM OFF THE ISLAND!"

But the most startling development at the convention took place about five minutes before adjournment. After a prayer that God would "give us grace seriously to lay to heart the great dangers we are in by our unhappy divisions," Bishop Duncan announced, after a brief consultation with the members of his standing committee, that he would invoke an obscure diocesan canon[5] that would have

4. Bishop Duncan's position regarding women in the priesthood has been inconsistent. Although he ordained women clergy and received them into his diocese, and indeed appointed at least two women clergy to prominent positions (Mary Hays as canon missioner and Catherine Brall as provost of the Cathedral), he nonetheless stated in a speech at Nashotah House Seminary that the question of women priests had not garnered consensus among Anglicans, and it was not a settled matter. He added that the ordination of women was a "new understanding," and it might take up to a hundred years before the matter is settled. He also expressed displeasure with the General Convention decision to make women's ordination mandatory (i.e., that ordination shall not be withheld on the basis of gender), on the grounds that the decision was a "repudiation of the consensus of Anglicanism." Also, many conservative clergy and laypersons, such as the Rev. Geoff Chapman, subscribe to a theory of "male primacy" when it came to women's ordination—the idea that women could be ordained, but that once ordained, should not hold positions of authority, such as rector or bishop.

5. XV, sec. 6: "The Convention may, by a two-thirds vote, dissolve its union with any Parish. Provided, however, that . . . notice of said proposed action shall have been given in the preceding Annual Convention." At the 2005 Convention, the bishop announced, almost sotto voce, that he would not proceed

the effect of dissolving the relationship between Calvary Church and the diocese and between St. Stephen's, Wilkinsburg, and the diocese. The reason these parishes had been singled out was that they were plaintiffs in the lawsuit against the bishop and other diocesan officers. The bishop declared that the congregations in question had acted in ways that were both unchristian and un-biblical, pointing out that St. Paul had admonished the faithful in Corinth to refrain from taking one another to court (1 Cor 6:1–8).[6] He went on to say that the canon "provides that the Convention may dissolve its connection to a parish in cases where there are egregious breaches of faith or church order.[7]

Such words are not found in the canon itself. Canons, more-over, are not capricious. Disciplinary canons always specify the offenses with which a person or other entity is charged, the means by which the charges may be aired in the appropriate tribunal, as well as the options at the disposal of that tribunal in the resolution

---

to remove the parishes from the diocese. He claimed this was because of events that had taken place since his original announcement, but I believe his change of heart was due to the fact that he had no canonical basis on which to proceed in the first place.

6. There is a certain irony and inconsistency in Bishop Duncan's claim that Christians ought not to sue one another in court. In 2001, the Rt. Rev. Jane Dixon, bishop of Washington, sued the Rev. Samuel Edwards, rector of Christ Church, Accokeek, Maryland, demanding that he step down as rector because he had refused to recognize her as bishop (on account of her gender) and because he would not give her a guarantee that he would keep Accokeek Parish in the Episcopal Church. At that time, Bishop Duncan, although not named in the suit as a party to either plaintiff or defendant, filed a "friend of the court" brief on behalf of Father Edwards (the court decided in favor of Bishop Dixon).

7 It is interesting to note another aspect of the bishop's strategy as re-gards this unprecedented and unjustifiable action. During a break prior to the bishop's announcement, the Rev. Douglas McGlynn, then president of the standing committee, approached me and asked if I could withdraw the lawsuit. I explained to Fr. McGlynn that (a) I was not predisposed to make such a move, and (b) even if I were, it was not a decision I could make unilaterally. Reportedly, both Fr. McGlynn and Bishop Duncan also approached the Rev. Diane Shepard, rector of St. Stephen's, Wilkinsburg, insisting that St. Stephen's drop the suit. She, too, informed them that she was not so disposed, and in any event could take no action without the concurrence of her vestry.

of the case. Absent such language, it is clear that the canon had no disciplinary intent at all.

Given that the basis of the lawsuit brought by the parishes was to uphold the constitution and canons of the Episcopal Church, the sudden attack against Calvary and St. Stephen's was consistent with the anti-national-church theme of diocesan convention. Our complaint, as has been pointed out, objected to the decision on the part of the bishop and diocesan officers to defy those canons, an action that they hoped would give to congregations who leave TEC the right to take with them the property they were occupying at the time of their departure.

Some observers of this development opined that there may have been another motivation on the part of the bishop for taking this action, namely to impress Archbishop Orombi. African prelates have far more power than their American counterparts, and it was not uncommon for African bishops to ask American bishops why they did not take stronger actions against clergy who were less than supportive of their bishops' agendas. The eviction notice handed down by Bishop Duncan may well have been delivered, in part, to make it appear that he could exercise the kind of power that was normative in African provinces of the Anglican Communion.

9

More Primatial Promulgations

THE FREQUENCY OF MEETINGS of the primates during the first decade of the twenty-first century serves as a reliable indicator that the Anglican Communion was indeed in crisis. In February of 2005, Archbishop Williams invited the heads of the Anglican provinces to meet together for the third time in less than two years. The venue was Dromantine, in Northern Ireland, and their host was Archbishop Robin Eames, the architect of the Windsor Report, and it was that report that was the principal focus of the gathering.

If, indeed, the Windsor Report attempted to appease those on both sides of the Anglican theological divide, the communiqué issued by the primates at Dromantine (thirty-five out of thirty-eight were present) continued in the same vein. While admitting, for example, that many primates were "alarmed" that the theological principle of Lambeth I.10 appeared to have been abandoned by the "developments in North America," the primatial statement made two important concessions. The first was that those developments "proceeded entirely in accordance with their constitutional processes and requirements." This point is of importance to us because it is at the core of our argument in the Calvary lawsuit, which maintained that Bishop Duncan had acted improperly because

Gene Robinson had been duly elected and consecrated in strict accordance with the constitution and canons of the Episcopal Church. As a bishop of that church, Duncan was not authorized to declare those events illegal, and subsequently to take actions that where inconsistent with the Episcopal Church's constitution and canons, in response to them. The second "primatial concession" is that the document upheld the principle of "pastoral support and care for homosexual people," and decried the victimization of such persons as "anathema to us."[1]

As we read on, however, we see that the primates lower the boom. In an effort to ensure that "the recommendations of the Windsor Report be properly addressed," the primates, in a delicately worded proposal, decided that in order to provide time for the American and Canadian churches to consider the Windsor Report's recommendations, they be asked to "voluntarily withdraw their members from the Anglican Consultative Council for the period leading up to the next Lambeth Conference" (2008). Furthermore, the Anglican Church of Canada and TEC were asked to send representatives to the Anglican Consultative Council's meeting in Nottingham in June, 2005, so that they "may have an opportunity to set out the thinking behind the recent actions of their Provinces."[2] Many observers saw this action as a classic Anglican compromise—between a blanket approval of the actions of the North American churches on the one hand (which message might have been conveyed through silence), and, on the other hand, a summary banishment of them from the governing bodies of Anglicanism.[3]

But the primates' actions may have had a more subtle but nonetheless serious effect. In response to the primates' invitation, TEC presented at the Nottingham meeting a document entitled

1. "Primates' Meeting Communiqué," February 24, 2005.

2. Ibid.

3. Bishop Duncan, however, saw the request through a different set of lenses: "The Episcopal Church has been asked to choose between repentance marked by a real returning to the Anglican mainstream, or walking apart from the rest of the Anglican Communion" (Episcopal Diocese of Pittsburgh website, http://www.episcopalpgh.org, February 25, 2005).

To Set Our Hope on Christ, in which, at the primates' request, they sought to explain how, in light of authority and Scripture as Anglicanism has received them, as well as "the apostolic tradition and reasoned reflection, a person living in a same gender union may be considered eligible to lead the flock of Christ."[4] Many had hoped that, in light of their compliance with the primates' request, TEC and the Anglican Church of Canada might be allowed to remain on the council. But the North Americans' eloquent apologia notwithstanding, the ACC, following the primates' recommendation, voted to suspend from its "official entities" the representatives of both churches until Lambeth 2008. The potential impact of that decision was analyzed by the Irish delegation to the ACC. They warned:

> Their churches are precluded from participation in other important decisions which could both enhance fellowship and create perspective . . . For the ACC, a genuinely synodical international gathering [the ACC being the only one of the four Instruments of Unity that includes priests and laypersons] to have its membership and atmosphere adjusted essentially at the behest of the Primates' Meeting would severely damage the balance of dispersed authority within Anglicanism.[5]

The Irish delegates go on to suggest that the Windsor Report may be a kind of Trojan horse, leading to a bishop- and archbishop-dominated "centralized curialization" of Anglicanism. Evidence of such a tendency was the ACC's decision to make primates *ex officio* members. That action increased the voting membership from 77 to 114 but, more significantly, decreased the proportion of lay members from one half to one third. The authors expressed the opinion that the actions of the ACC, by removing North Americans and increasing primatial participation, had the

---

4. The Most Rev. Frank T. Griswold, in Battle et al., *To Set Our Hope on Christ*, Foreword.

5. Church of Ireland. "Irish Anglican Consultative Council (ACC)," February 26, 2005.

effect of cementing divisions and compromising the independence of the ACC.[6]

It would appear that during this testy period of Anglican and Episcopal history, there existed a tendency toward a knee-jerk reaction to solve problems by simply removing the offending party. This seemed to be the remedy locally, as in the case with the threatened ouster of two parishes in the Diocese of Pittsburgh; nationally, as evidenced by the movement toward "realignment"; and now internationally, as was the case with the North American churches being asked to step down from the ACC. These actions bespoke a new, post-Windsor brand of Anglicanism, which is more contractual than it is covenantal, more rigid than supple. As I observed elsewhere:

> the Anglican Communion in this post-Windsor era seems to be characterized by distrust . . . To many, human sexuality has become the quintessential litmus test, and the views of individuals, parishes, dioceses or provinces on that issue determine their fitness for membership. Our default position seems to be changing from a propensity to being inclusive to a tendency to remove from Anglican fellowship those who do not meet the standard of "orthodoxy."[7]

The primates at Dromantine, as they attempted to commend the Windsor Report as a "way forward" for the Communion, reportedly had problems going forward themselves. Archbishop Akinola of Nigeria sent a letter to the Archbishop of Canterbury indicating that he and his fellow GAFCON prelates would not

---

6. This harkens back to a resolution passed at Lambeth 1998, at which bishops were urged to exercise greater leadership, through their "moral authority" in defining the limits of Anglican diversity on "doctrinal, moral and pastoral matters," including possible intervention in internally troubled provinces. Ian Douglas raised questions about the resolution on the grounds that it "gives the Primates' Meeting . . . unheard of extra-metropolitical authority to intervene in the life of Anglican provinces locally, while eviscerating the sharing of power with lay people and priests in the ACC" (Hassett, *Anglican Communion in Crisis*, 118).

7. Lewis, "Covenant, Contract and Communion," 601ff.

share the fellowship of the Eucharist with Presiding Bishop Frank Griswold. When Dr. Williams offered to appoint others who would celebrate, Akinola responded that it was not a matter of the unworthiness of the minister, but a conviction that unity of belief should precede unity of worship. It was not a question of receiving "from" the presiding bishop, but "with" him, that is, at the same service. (This incident followed one in which objections were made to Bishop Griswold being the preacher at a service in Belfast prior to the Primates' Meeting, because a primate "representing the historic teaching on human sexuality" had not been invited![8])

It is tragic to note, too, that the presiding bishop, at a meeting of the House of Bishops held two weeks after the adjournment of the primates' gathering, identified by name six Episcopalians, among them Bishop Duncan, who had influenced the course of the Primates' Meeting. They reportedly had arranged to stay at a nearby hotel, from which they communicated electronically with certain primates.[9]

Such were the tumultuous developments on the other side of the Atlantic that affected, directly and indirectly, our struggles in the Diocese of Pittsburgh.

8. "PB's Choice to Preach in Belfast Doubted," February 25, 2005.
9. "Primates 'Out for Blood at Meeting,'" March 15, 2005.

10

A Ceasefire!

THE LAWSUIT THAT WAS in many ways the centerpiece of the convention at Moon Township wended its way through the courts. After several fits and starts, involving a variety of legal maneuvers, and including attempts on the part of the defendants to dismiss the case entirely, we arrived at a point at which it appeared that the matter was resolved to the satisfaction of both plaintiffs and defendants. In October 2005, the court approved a "stipulation" agreed to by counsel for both plaintiffs and defendants, which, it is important to note, carried the weight of an injunction, binding all parties. The stipulation made the following points:

1. **Property held by the diocese:** In a section that upheld the provisions of the Dennis Canon, the stipulation declared that even if "a majority of the parishes in the Diocese might decide not to remain in the Episcopal Church of the United States of America" (as turned out to be the case after "realignment" became effective in 2008), property "held or administered by the Episcopal Diocese of Pittsburgh of the Episcopal Church of the United States of America" for the beneficial use of the parishes and institutions of the diocese shall continue to be so held. Otherwise put, those parishes, however few in number,

that opted to remain part of the Episcopal Church would, in fact, constitute the Episcopal Church in the Diocese of Pittsburgh, and would be entitled to the use of real property, such as Calvary Camp,[1] and personal property, such as diocesan endowment funds and other assets. The significance of this aspect of the stipulation cannot be overemphasized, as the "Anglican" Diocese of Pittsburgh, even after secession, continued to maintain that they are the "true" and bona fide diocese, because a majority of the congregations had voted for "realignment."

2. **Property held by parishes**: Importantly, the settlement established that any parishes electing to disaffiliate from the diocese must follow a process that provides for openness and rights of both participation and objection by all interested parties. A key provision is the requirement that notification of desired disaffiliation be sent to all members of the parish in question, the bishop, the board of trustees of the diocese, and the rector and vestry of every parish in the diocese.

3. **The Network**: Another important provision in the settlement is that any parish that does not want to be a member of the Network of Anglican Dioceses and Parishes (membership that had been "conferred" by fiat on all parishes in the diocese) may withdraw from the network by notifying the bishop and the board of trustees.

4. **Resolution 6 of the 2003 diocesan convention**: This section of the stipulation is perhaps the most significant, as it declares that Resolution 6, "Title to Property," the initial diocesan action to which we objected in the lawsuit, *"has been withdrawn and is of no effect."*

5. **Amendment of Article I, Section 1, of the diocesan constitution at the 2004 convention**: That amendment to the

---

1. Sheldon Calvary Camp was founded in 1936 as a camp for the boys in Calvary's choir. It later became coed and open to children from other congregations and indeed from the greater Pittsburgh community. In more recent years, ownership was conveyed to the Episcopal Diocese of Pittsburgh.

diocesan constitution had stated that in cases where the provisions of the constitution and canons of the diocese or resolutions of its convention disagree with those of constitution and canons of the national church or its General Convention, the local determination shall prevail. *The stipulation asserts that this has absolutely no bearing on matters pertaining to property.*[2]

6. **Calvary's Escrow Account:** In a previous stipulation, the court had ordered that the funds that Calvary would normally have paid to the diocese as its assessment, which amounted to nearly $250,000 for the term of the litigation, be placed instead in an escrow account.[3] Under the settlement, $50,000 of this amount was paid to the diocese, while the balance was returned to Calvary. If so determined by Calvary, such funds might be applied to legal costs.[4]

The decision was hailed as a victory not only for Calvary Church and the people of the Diocese of Pittsburgh whose rights we fought to protect, but for the Episcopal Church as a whole. Already our litigation, we believed, had served to dissuade other dioceses whose bishops had contemplated secession, by demonstrating to them that they might well suffer consequences on account of their actions. But our efforts also served as encouragement for the

---

2. We also believed that this amendment to the diocesan Constitution was similarly improper when applied to ecclesiastical matters, but that is an issue not typically addressed by civil courts, and therefore not covered by the settlement.

3. Defendants agreed to this stipulation, which specified that "payment into escrow by Plaintiff Calvary of funds due and payable to the Diocese shall be treated as payment to the Diocese of such funds . . . for any and all purposes related to the good standing, rights, responsibilities, and/or privileges of the Plaintiff Calvary as a member of the Diocese." Nevertheless, the bishop, treasurer, and other diocesan personnel publicly criticized Calvary Parish for "withholding" funds from the diocese, and laid at Calvary's door the blame for the reduction in diocesan programmatic initiatives.

4. It should be acknowledged that Calvary received contributions toward its legal costs from several sources, notably individuals and parishes in the Diocese of Pittsburgh, bishops and clergy from other dioceses, and member parishes of the Consortium of Endowed Episcopal Parishes.

other "reorganizing" dioceses that had experienced the pains of secession. We had taken actions that, we hoped, were appropriate to protect the principles now reflected in the court-approved settlement.

It must be understood that the stipulation, agreed to by all parties, was the long-desired result of the legal action by Calvary Church. The stipulation vindicated Calvary's claims, including the validity of the Dennis Canon (although according to the wording of the stipulation, no party admitted any wrongdoing).

But all was not at ease in Zion. Although the court papers described the resolution outlined in the stipulation as "amicable," it became clear to us that the defendants were not at all pleased. This stipulation may have resulted in a change in strategy on the part of Bishop Duncan and his allies, but not a change in goal. The secessionists were still very much bound and determined to establish a parallel church, which they believed would be faithful to the historic faith and order of the church catholic, and which, they hoped, would supplant the Episcopal Church and be recognized as the only legitimate community of Anglicans in the United States. Moreover, despite the unambiguous wording of the settlement, it was clear that the defendants had not abandoned the idea that they could somehow lay claim to the assets of the Diocese of Pittsburgh to aid them in their task, and therefore would seek to use the courts or other avenues to achieve their end. In short, this was not the end of the matter.

11

The Plot Thickens

IN NOVEMBER, 2005, LESS than a month after the settlement of the lawsuit, the "coming of age" celebration of the Anglican Communion Network of Dioceses and Parishes took place in Pittsburgh, in the form of a conference entitled "Hope and a Future."[1] The Network, which had come into being at a conference in Plano, Texas, in January 2004,[2] and whose moderator was Robert Duncan, was going great guns. Its key contention was a

1. The conference organizers took their theme from Jeremiah 29:11: "'For I know the plans I have for you,' declares the Lord, 'plans to prosper you and not to harm you, plans to give you hope and a future.'"

2. Founders of the Network have long contended that it was founded at the behest, indeed the express recommendation of Rowan Williams, Archbishop of Canterbury, during an informal meeting between the Archbishop and four conservative American bishops (Robert Duncan, Pittsburgh; Daniel Herzog, Albany; John Howe, Central Florida; and Jack Iker, Fort Worth). The meeting reportedly took place in London in October 2003, when a special meeting of the primates was held to discuss the implications of the then impending consecration of Canon V. Gene Robinson. In a report to the Diocese of Pittsburgh at Ascension Church, Pittsburgh, on October 19, 2003, Bishop Duncan informed those in attendance that what was then envisioned as the Network of Confessing Dioceses and Parishes "has Archbishop Rowan's encouragement." An ACC press release dated December 17, 2003, announcing the inaugural meeting of the Network stated, "The Network was formed last month at the suggestion of the Archbishop of Canterbury."

claim that it adhered to traditional, orthodox Christian doctrine on subjects such as the infallibility of Scripture and sexual morality (especially regarding the ordination of non-celibate homosexuals and the blessing of same-sex unions). Its headquarters were on the ninth floor of the Oliver Building in downtown Pittsburgh, conveniently situated down the hall from the new headquarters of the Episcopal Diocese of Pittsburgh—the bishop having moved from his suite of offices in Trinity Cathedral House half a block away.[3] Several greater and lesser prelates—many of them archbishops from the Global South, including Drexel Gomez of the West Indies, Emmanuel Kolini of Rwanda, and Henry Luke Orombi from Uganda—were in attendance, but it was clear that the most honored guest was Peter Jasper Akinola, archbishop of Nigeria, whose province claimed some eighteen million faithful, or nearly one out of every five Anglicans on the planet.

Akinola drew the line in the sand. He challenged American Anglicans to make a choice between the Network and the Episcopal Church, making it abundantly clear in his challenge that they were separate and distinct entities. Realignment (CAN-speak for "secession") was necessary because the Network, according to him, upheld biblical truth, which TEC had long abandoned. The irony of CAN's claims of the supremacy of Scripture is that it is quintessentially un-Anglican, smacking, as it does, of the *sola Scriptura* approach of the continental reformers, which Anglicans rejected in favor of an appeal to tradition and reason, as well as Scripture. In his *Laws of Ecclesiastical Polity*, Richard Hooker, Anglicanism's chief apologist, often credited with having come up with the "three-legged stool" of Anglicanism—Scripture, tradition, and reason—writes that "while the fundamental truths of the Christian faith are obvious even to the unlearned, the Bible as a whole is not evident [but] requires the use of 'theological reason.'"[4]

---

3. At the time of the move, the bishop announced that by procuring office space in a commercial building the diocese could make a "witness to the city." Many opined that the real reason was that when secession took place he would not be in the awkward position of occupying church property.

4. Cited in Lewis, *Church for the Future*, 98.

At this conference, moderator Duncan built on Akinola's challenge, and categorically stated, "there's no way for these two conflicted faiths to live under the same roof." He went a step further by saying that Episcopalians, therefore, had to choose between Jesus and "something less or a counterfeit. And we really think that counterfeit is what is being offered by the Episcopal Church at the moment." He was fully cognizant of the fact that people might wonder why he wished to remain bishop in a church that was counterfeit, and added that "there are those who will try to remove me here, as bishop of Pittsburgh."

Throughout the conference, Duncan made statements and committed acts that I and others believed were grounds for his being removed as bishop of Pittsburgh. One such act was his request of the bishop of Bolivia to ordain a priest who would be dispatched by Duncan. Not only was this a breach of TEC canon law, but of the Windsor Report ban on bishops encroaching on other jurisdictions. The fact that the Diocese of Pittsburgh had in its recent convention "submitted" to the Windsor Report made the act the more egregious.

STEEPLE OR PEOPLE?

Of particular interest to our lawsuit were the comments made at the conference by the Rev. Rick Warren, pastor of a conservative megachurch community, Saddleback Church in Lake Forest, California, and author of a best-selling book entitled *The Purpose-Driven Life*. He urged dissident Episcopalians to break with the Episcopal Church and to ignore the dispute over ownership of church property: "What's more important is your faith, not your facilities," he told the crowd at the Pittsburgh Convention Center. "The Church is people, not the steeple. They might get the building, but you get the blessing."[5] Meanwhile, back at the Court of Common Pleas in Pittsburgh, Bishop Duncan's newly hired team

5. Banerjee, "Conservative Episcopalians Warn Church," November 12, 2005,

of lawyers took positions indicating that the defendants retained an interest in the steeple, as we shall see below.

Because of a series of actions on the part of the defendants, a petition by the plaintiffs requesting that the court enforce the settlement order of October 2005 was filed in late December 2006, in conjunction with a request to expedite discovery, that is, a demand that the defendants produce certain documents (that would provide evidence that the plaintiffs' allegations were correct) within a shorter period of time than usual.[6]

REJECTION OF THE PRIMATE AND WITHDRAWAL FROM PROVINCE III

It was because we became aware of certain efforts on the part of the diocesan leadership that a request was made of the court to enforce the stipulation that had been agreed upon in the prior year. The matters addressed were not, as Bishop Duncan suggested in his pastoral letter on the subject, "theological and ecclesiastical [and] nothing to do with the property of the Diocese."[7] The petition cites specifically the decisions of the bishop and a majority of the standing committee to reject the leadership of the duly elected presiding bishop and primate of the Episcopal Church, Katharine Jefferts Schori, and to withdraw from Province III of the Episcopal Church.[8] These acts were tantamount, in our opinion, to removing property from the Episcopal Church since "the Diocese, through

6. Plaintiffs deemed it imperative that such discovery be delivered to the court prior to the beginning of the Primates' Meeting, scheduled for mid-February, as it was believed that Bishop Duncan could use that occasion to launch another aspect of his plan.

7. Duncan, "Pastoral Letter," January 29, 2007.

8. TEC is divided into nine (internal) geographical provinces (not to be confused with the thirty-eight provinces of the Anglican Communion, of which the entire Episcopal Church is one). Each province elects representatives to the executive council of TEC, which administers church affairs between General Conventions; and there is a bishop from each of the provinces on the presiding bishop's Council of Advice. The provinces also serve as courts of appeals for clergy who have been charged with canonical offenses.

its officers and by decisions of its convention, deemed itself no longer responsible to or a constituent part of the established canonical structures of the Church."

In response to our filing, Bishop Duncan issued a statement criticizing our actions. On December 21, he stated that there had been no breaches of the settlement agreement, and that he and his fellow defendants "fully expect to defeat this effort." He added: "It is a sad thing to see Calvary Church, which over the years has been part of so much that was good in the diocese, once again to attempt to use the secular legal system as a lever to enforce its own version of being Episcopalian on the majority here."[9]

In conveying these thoughts, the bishop of Pittsburgh seemed to have overlooked three important facts: first, that the basis of our petition was a stipulation to which he, through his counsel, gave his consent; second, that said stipulation was drawn up in a secular court; and third, that "our version" of the Episcopal Church was one based on a recognition of the authority of the duly elected presiding bishop and the decisions of General Convention. And while we were outnumbered in our own diocese, we were certainly part of the majority of the Episcopal Church. Although Bishop Duncan went on to assure his followers, even using language similar to that of the Dennis Canon, that "the property of the Episcopal Diocese of Pittsburgh will continue to be held and administered for the beneficial use of the parishes and institutions of the Diocese," it must be remembered that he was writing about a fictional diocesan structure called the Episcopal Diocese of Pittsburgh which in his mind would be part of the "realigned" church.

PLAINTIFF'S CHARGES

Among the salient charges made by the Plaintiffs were the following:[10]

9. Schjonberg, "Pittsburgh: Parish Asks Court," December 22, 2006.

10. Summary of proceedings and all quotations cited in this section are taken from the contents of the pleadings, or minutes of the hearing on the motion to expedite discovery, held in the Court of Common Pleas, Allegheny

1. The dissemination of the Chapman memo outlining a plan to facilitate the transference of diocesan assets;

2. The diocesan standing committee's June 2006 request for "immediate alternative primatial oversight and pastoral care," which was ratified by the November diocesan convention, for creating a "replacement" jurisdiction for North America;

3. A decision of the bishop and a majority of the standing committee to withdraw from Province III;

4. The decision of the diocesan convention to cut off all funds designated for the national church;

5. The fact that the defendants, despite their having effectively separated themselves from TEC, had access to the assets that rightly belong to the Episcopal Diocese, including a multimillion-dollar endowment fund that could be used for purposes not consistent with the mission of TEC.

Counsel argued that inasmuch as Bishop Duncan had "withdrawn from the organizational structures" of the Church, it would appear that "he isn't in the Episcopal Church for any purpose at all except his claim that he is." In an address to the defendants' counsel, the court ruled that "the rightness or the wrongness of who's withdrawing and who's staying is irrelevant to me, but the fact that somebody is withdrawing is relevant because now you are in the facility that belongs to the Episcopal Church of North America and you are no longer affiliated with the Episcopal Church of North America. If that is discovered to be true, then you violated the terms of the consent order and there's a question whether the churches are evicted, will have to pay rent or some other remedy which Mr. DeForest's clients would have."

After weighing all the arguments, the court ordered that the defendants should deliver the requested documents by January 9, 2007, a mere two weeks after the motion was heard. After issuing the order, the court iterated that the matter was "germane to the issue of the title to this property [and] the and the use of this

County, PA, December 22, 2006.

property by someone other than a member of the North American Episcopal Church." This statement underscored the stated purpose of Calvary's original complaint in equity.

DEFENDANTS' CHARGES AND PLAINTIFFS' RESPONSE

In February 2007, the defendants filed a motion to dismiss the petition to enforce the stipulation. Their grounds were complex. The defendants alleged, for example, that the court did not have jurisdiction to enforce the terms of the stipulation. But the objections of particular relevance are the following:

a. The petition's allegations nowhere allege facts that, if true, constitute a breach of the stipulation; rather, plaintiffs outline a series of allegations relating to a theological dispute within the Episcopal Church and the Anglican Communion.

b. The petition's allegations and claims relating to the rights of the Episcopal Church of the United States are improper because TEC is not a party to the stipulation.

c. The petition is also improper in that it asserts claims arising out of speeches regarding matters of faith and/or statements made by the defendants. Such claims cannot be the basis of any court adjudication since such speech and statements are protected by the First and Fourteenth Amendments to the U.S. Constitution.

In summary, the defendants argued that this was a religious or theological dispute, and therefore not within the province of the court; that the plaintiffs had no standing to argue the case on behalf of the Episcopal Church because the Episcopal Church was not a plaintiff; and lastly that statements by Bishop Duncan and others could not be used as evidence of violation of the stipulation, since they were protected by the Constitution's amendments that guarantee free speech and equal protection under the law. Among the more salient arguments made by the plaintiffs in opposition were the following:

1. The plaintiffs are not seeking adjudication of ecclesiastical matters, but rather pursuant to neutral principle of law.

2. The contention on the part of the defendants that their rights of free speech, under federal and state Constitutions, have been denied, is absurd. Nothing in either the U.S. or Pennsylvania Constitution implies that a person's public or private statements cannot be evidence against them as to their intent and actions.

On May 8, 2007, the court ordered that the defendants' motion to dismiss the petition be denied. We were making steady, albeit not rapid, progress.

12

Even More Primatial Promulgations

AS 2007 DAWNED, THE tension between the conservative and progressive camps had increased considerably—not only in the Diocese of Pittsburgh, where Calvary and Bishop Duncan had endured another round of court battles, but within TEC and throughout the Anglican Communion. The American and Canadian churches at this time were in a kind of limbo, since as a result of their actions (the consecration of Gene Robinson and the approval of same-sex blessings) they had been reduced to "observer status" on the Anglican Consultative Council. But the most ominous cloud looming over the Communion was the Primates' Meeting scheduled to take place in February in Dar-es-Salaam, Tanzania.

Much was riding on that meeting. The secessionists had long hoped that the primates of the Global South would function as *dei ex machina*, to miraculously emerge on the stage of Anglicanism, sort things out, and ensure "an happy issue" out of all the church's affliction. In this connection, the bishop and standing committee of the Diocese of Pittsburgh laid two major requests before that body. First, that the primates reject the authority of Katharine Jefferts Schori as presiding bishop of TEC, on the grounds that she "teaches a manifestly defective Christology as well as embraces moral actions and teachings directly contrary to the Windsor Report."[1] Second, in addition to appointing an alternative primate in her stead, who would be "an antidote to the inherent independence of action that has characterized relationships among bishops and dioceses," the Pittsburgh diocese asked that there be created a new "permanent Anglican identity in the U.S.," namely a jurisdiction made up exclusively of dioceses in the Network that would be separate and distinct from TEC, wile enjoying the universal recognition of the Communion, thus fulfilling the "prophecy" contained in the Chapman memo.

It is unclear whether Bishop Duncan really believed that the primates, much less the Global South primates, who have little or no power outside of their respective provinces, could bring about such radical changes in the Church's structure. Jurisdictional matters, such as the establishment of new provinces, fall under the purview of the Anglican Consultative Council, and even the ACC has no authority to remove the duly elected primate of an autonomous province. Indeed, according to the then chair of the ACC, Archbishop John Paterson, the Pittsburgh request might well have fallen into the category of constitutional changes, which would require a two-thirds vote of the entire Communion—an unrealistic expectation. Despite the sound and fury of the Global South primates and other conservative voices, the majority of the Communion, according to Paterson, was still desirous of its remaining intact.[2]

It is my opinion that Bishop Duncan had no realistic expectations that he could be successful in convincing the primates and other entities to effect such herculean accomplishments. Nor, in my view, could he have reasonably expected that the presiding bishop and the General Convention would consent, willy-nilly, to the evisceration of their canonical authority, which they were being asked to cede to foreign prelates outside of TEC.

1. "Request for Alternative Primatial Oversight," November 6, 2006.

2. Conversation between the author and Archbishop Paterson during the meeting of the Advisory Council to the Anglican Observer to the United Nations, Lambeth Palace, February 6, 2007.

The long awaited Primates' Meeting in Tanzania started off on a sour note, itself indicative of the level of distrust among Anglicans, which the primates' communiqué would recognize at the meeting's end. At least seven Global South primates, including Akinola of Nigeria, Kolini of Rwanda, Orombi of Uganda and Venables of the Southern Cone, refused to receive communion at the opening Eucharist with Presiding Bishop Katharine Jefferts Schori "because," as Archbishop Orombi wrote to his people, "to do so would be a violation of Scriptural teaching and the traditional Anglican understanding."[3]

The communiqué made reference to a tension in the Communion, a tension "so deep that the fabric of our common life together has been torn,"[4] and laid the blame squarely at the door of the Episcopal Church. Mention was also made of the problems caused by episcopal interventions—that is, the practice whereby bishops performed sacramental acts in other provinces or dioceses, especially the consecration of other bishops, without the permission of the local authority. But the theological and political bias of the primates' report could be seen in the comments it offered about those interventions. It iterated a point made in the Windsor Report, that there was not a "moral equivalence" between the "innovations" of ordination of a partnered gay bishop and the authorization of same sex-blessings on the one hand, and episcopal interventions on the other, "since the cross-boundary interventions arose from a deep concern for the welfare of Anglicans in the face of innovation"[5]—a statement that comes very close to condoning and justifying those interventions. Further support of the interventions is suggested in

3. Orombi, "Archbishop of Uganda on the Primates Meeting," February 21, 2007. In his letter, the archbishop also indicated that he refused to receive Holy Communion at the previous Primates' Meeting, in Ireland, owing to the presence of presiding Bishop Griswold. While no scriptural or theological source was cited, the subsequent action in Tanzania was likely taken because Orombi and several of his fellow primates objected to the presiding bishop's presence as the embodiment of a province that was teaching false doctrine. Bishop Jefferts Schori's gender was doubtless another factor.

4. "Primates' Meeting Communiqué," February 19, 2007, ¶9.

5. Ibid., ¶10.

paragraph 32, where we read, "Those of us who have intervened in other jurisdictions believe that we cannot abandon those who have appealed to us for pastoral care in situations in which they find themselves at odds with the normal jurisdiction."

There was ample evidence throughout the communiqué that the primates lacked a sense of understanding of the nature of TEC, or otherwise put, had a skewed understanding of it. The communiqué presumably allowed for the "listening process," a mechanism established by Lambeth 1998 for listening to the experiences of homosexual persons, but seemed not to recognize that TEC has been through such a process and that clergy and people of TEC had taken steps in faithful response to what they learned. The report repeatedly iterates the Lambeth Resolution I.10, and refers to it as "accepted" teaching, when it in fact is a non-binding opinion of a majority of Anglican bishops.[6] What is notably absent from the communiqué and the Windsor Report is the "Lambeth Principle," a decision to "agree to disagree," which governed the Church's response to the no less acrimonious debate over women's ordination.[7]

The primates' view of the American Church is perhaps most telling in paragraph 27, in which they acknowledge that a number of TEC bishops "are unable in conscience to accept the primacy" of their presiding bishop. Their statement, "At the same time we

6. Lambeth I.10 is the widely publicized resolution on human sexuality passed by the 1998 Lambeth Conference. It rejected homosexual practice as "incompatible with Scripture," and declared that it "cannot advise the legitimizing of same sex unions nor ordaining those involved in same gender unions."

7. Sometimes called "reception," the Lambeth Principle is a means whereby the Lambeth Conference consciously created a way for provinces to opt for different courses of actions while demonstrating mutual respect. The principle has been used most frequently when Lambeth has been faced with controversial issues, such as the ordination of women. In that instance, there was an agreement that if Province A ordains women and Province B does not, Province B recognizes Province A's right to ordain women, and Province A does not condemn Province B for not doing so. Sometimes the principle is observed through a period of discernment, during which provinces will try to maintain the fullest communion possible when some churches fail to accept or remain uncertain about the charges (see Lewis, *Church for the Future*, 95).

recognize that the Presiding Bishop has been duly elected in accordance with the Constitution and Canons of the Episcopal Church, which must be respected," might be understood to convey the notion that the primates would be willing to be instrumental in the removal of the authority of the presiding bishop if they could. In point of fact, the recommendation that a committee be established whose role it would be to "negotiate the necessary structures for pastoral care" (i.e., to arrange alternative episcopal oversight in TEC) can be seen as effecting the same end. Known as the "pastoral council," it would be made up of five primates, three of whom would be nominated by entities outside the Episcopal Church (the primates and the Archbishop of Canterbury), an arrangement that would have the effect of minimizing or even eradicating the authority of the presiding bishop in her own province.

As Calvary's junior warden observed, the primates' plan was seriously flawed for at least two reasons:

> First, contrary to what the Primates appear to believe [the plan] will exacerbate rather than heal the current divisions within TEC. Second, by singling out TEC as uniquely deserving of extra-Provincial supervision and (potentially) discipline, the Primates have made it harder rather than easier for TEC to engage in the covenant process. It is hard to see how a purportedly neutral process can succeed when one Province out of the 38 is being asked to cede important aspects of its autonomy before the covenant is even put in place.[8]

Finally, since these pages are principally concerned with discussing the matter of the lawsuit filed by Calvary against Robert Duncan et al., we should say that of particular interest to us is a comment in paragraph 25 of the communiqué: "So great has been the estrangement between some of the faithful and the Episcopal Church that this has led to recrimination, hostility and even to disputes in the civil courts." While no one denies the existence of passionate feelings, it was not these emotions that drove us to

8. Ayres, "Some Reflections on the Primates' Communiqué," February 24, 2007.

THE RECENT UNPLEASANTNESS

court, but issues arising from the rule of law. The primates' line of reasoning led to an unacceptable recommendation that "representatives of the Episcopal Church and of those congregations in property disputes with it to suspend all actions in law arising from this situation."[9] This recommendation may have been influenced by Bishop Duncan, who was present at the meeting at the request of the Archbishop of Canterbury, along with other American bishops, to present, together with the presiding bishop, different perspectives on the situation in the American Church. Not surprisingly, since suspension of the lawsuit in Pittsburgh would have been favorable and beneficial to his cause, Bishop Duncan, upon his return, appealed to the primates' recommendation in a speech to the diocese in which he said, "If they [the Plaintiffs] had a shred of integrity, they would drop the lawsuit immediately."[10]

It should be clear to us by now that the complaint in equity filed by Calvary Church in the autumn of 2003 had a profound effect on the life of the Church far beyond the borders of Allegheny County, Pennsylvania.

9. "Primates' Meeting Communiqué," February 19, 2007, section "On Property Disputes."

10. Address to laypersons and clergy in the Diocese of Pittsburgh, St. Martin's, Monroeville, February 24, 2007.

13

"By Schisms Rent Asunder, by Heresies Distressed"

THE PRIMATES' PROPOSAL WAS, wisely and predictably, rejected by the House of Bishops when it convened at Camp Allen, Texas, in March 2007, the month following the Primates' Meeting in Dar-es-Salaam. Since Bishop Duncan and his followers had made it clear that the implementation of the proposed scheme for alternative primatial oversight as outlined in the primates' communiqué was the only one acceptable to him and his fellow separatists, they were forced to reassess their situation. To that end, a retreat of the diocesan leadership—bishops, standing committee, diocesan council, and board of trustees—was held in May 2007. Duncan opened the gathering by stating, "We're here together . . . to discuss our way forward in light of our failure to obtain Alternative Primatial Oversight." Then followed a curious statement, given that there should not have been any realistic expectation that the primates' APO plan would be accepted: "We are facing something that we never thought we would face. We thought we would prevail. We thought that what we believed and what the majority of the Communion believed would be provided for."[1]

1. Virtue, "Pittsburgh Bishop Faces Critical Moment," July 26, 2007.

The diocesan leaders, with the help of a consultant, considered four options for the diocese: a) to continue on its present course, with the result that it would remain "at the periphery of the Episcopal Church"; b) "submit to the will of TEC," which would necessitate reversing the actions of diocesan conventions over the past four years; c) attempt to separate as a diocese from the Episcopal Church; or d) attempt to create space for parishes to negotiate an exit from the diocese. Options a, b, and d were rejected, and the diocesan leadership voted to bring to fruition that for which the groundwork had long existed—schism between the Diocese of Pittsburgh and the Episcopal Church.

As news of this decision spread around the diocese, it did not sit well with many of the faithful, who had taken Bishop Duncan at his word that he was advocating for an *ecclesia reformanda*, a new, improved church, as it were, which would undergo a process of reformation from within. They believed him, too, when he indicated that neither he nor they would ever have to leave the Episcopal Church. Now, poised for flight, many laypeople and clergy in the diocese were loath to imagine affiliation with some (as yet to be identified) fellowship of Anglicans in another part of the world. Indeed, they were concerned that they would no longer be Episcopalians, or even Anglicans, since dissident bishops and their flocks were not recognized by the ACC, and therefore, strictly speaking, no longer in communion with the See of Canterbury.[2] And then, for Episcopalians suffering from an "edifice complex," there was the question of church property. Would acceptance of Duncan's plan to leave TEC mean that heretofore faithful Episcopalians now caught up in this theological and jurisdictional maelstrom would be forced to give up their parish buildings?

---

2. For example, Martyn Mimms, former rector of Truro Parish, Virginia, was consecrated by the archbishop of Nigeria and then installed by him as Archbishop of the Convocation of Anglicans in North America (CANA), headquartered in Fairfax, Virginia. Mimms was not recognized by the bishop of Virginia, the presiding bishop, or the Archbishop of Canterbury; nor was CANA recognized by the ACC.

Such reservations notwithstanding, a resolution was passed overwhelmingly[3] at the 142nd diocesan convention, held in Johnstown in November 2007. Containing the requisite changes to the diocesan constitution and canons to purportedly make separation from TEC a possibility, it only awaited the concurring decision at the 2008 convention to be officially enacted. To presage, perhaps, his own imminent departure from the Episcopal fold, Duncan announced that the convention banquet speaker at the Eucharist would be the Rt. Rev. John Guernsey. A deposed priest from the Diocese of Virginia, he was consecrated in Uganda weeks before the convention and was sent back to the United States to minister to former Episcopalians who deemed themselves to be under the spiritual care of an African archbishop. His presence was therefore an affront to faithful Episcopalians in the diocese. The *Wall Street Journal* described Guernsey as an "offshore bishop."[4] Archbishop Orombi had a more flowery moniker for Guernsey: "Biblically orthodox domestic ecclesial entity in the U.S.A."[5] The supreme irony is that, at a convention whose delegates would be asked to vote to realign themselves with those who are in communion with the See of Canterbury, the guest speaker and preacher is one who was not recognized by the See of Canterbury.

It became apparent that, in the aftermath of convention, some clergy and laity had decided that they would not join Bishop Duncan in his exodus from TEC. This became even clearer on

3. The vote was a vote "by orders," which means that clergy and laity voted separately—normally a requirement for constitutional and canonical changes. The results were: clergy, 109 yes, 24 no, 0 abstentions (67 needed to pass); laity, 118 yes, 58 no, 1 abstention (87 needed to pass). The degree of success of the measure at this convention, and even at the next, was due in part to the fact that newly enacted canons of the diocese had created an enlarged diocese with porous boundaries, enabling clergy and laypeople from out-of-state parishes to cast a vote. Also, the recent "planting" of several parishes throughout the diocese also served to increase the ranks of the electorate. Some parishes were admitted to convention in 2008, and voted to secede from the Episcopal Church at the same convention!

4. Higgins, "Episcopal Church Dissidents Seek Authority Overseas," September 20, 2007.

5. Orombi, letter to "Rectors, Clergy and Lay Leaders," June 22, 2007.

January 30, 2008 when an article appeared in the *Pittsburgh Post-Gazette* entitled, "Letter Shows Rift among Episcopal Conservatives," which reported that twelve clergy, identified in the article as "theologically conservative clergy in the Diocese of Pittsburgh," stated unequivocally that they would not join in Duncan's departure from the Episcopal Church.[6] One of the "Gang of Twelve," as the group became known, the Rev. Scott Quinn, rector of Nativity, Crafton, plainly stated: "The bishop has made a mistake; he seems to be going in a different direction than we are." The Rev. Jay Geisler, then rector of St. Stephen's, McKeesport, observed that they were unified with the bishop on a vision, but not unified on a tactic. The authors of the one-paragraph letter made it clear that, while they supported the reformation of the Episcopal Church, they "have determined to remain within, and not realign out of it." The priests' letter to Bishop Duncan marked a distinct point of divergence. Moreover, according to the Rev. Jeffrey Murph, rector of St. Thomas' Church, Oakmont, and one of the signatories, trust for their father-in-God had eroded, mainly because they believed that he had reneged on his statement to them that he would not leave the Episcopal Church.

The clergy and people of the diocese who were thus disappointed cannot be blamed for not having understood Duncan's nuanced statement, which was, I believe, predicated, in turn, on a rather complex ecclesiology. Since, according to his thinking, the Episcopal Church had exceeded its authority by approving such "innovations" as same-sex blessings and the ordination of non-celibate gay bishops, it had ceased being the Episcopal Church, leaving that distinction to those like himself, who, Duncan averred, faithfully proclaimed "the faith once delivered to the saints." Therefore, Duncan could contend that wherever he and his followers went became the Episcopal Church in its new epitomization, or otherwise put, was the *continuation* of the "true" Episcopal Diocese of Pittsburgh.[7] This is why Duncan, on the eve of his

6. Levin, "Letter Shows Rift among Episcopal Conservatives," January 30, 2008.

7. Duncan's ecclesiology is summed up in his "Special Convention Address"

election as the first bishop of the so-called Anglican Diocese of Pittsburgh, could declare, "I am deeply grateful for the possibility of serving as both the seventh and eighth bishop of the Episcopal Diocese of Pittsburgh."[8] This is why the first convention of the new Anglican diocese was advertised as its 144th! Such a line of reasoning, however, as we would soon learn, did not succeed in convincing the courts.

The twelve signatories were emphatic, however, that leaving the Duncan camp did not necessarily signal a change in their theological views. They remained opposed to same-sex unions and the ordination of gay clergy, for example, but unlike Bishop Duncan, who declared in his convention address that we had reached "a fork in the road" precluding the possibility that those with differing views could remain in the same spiritual house, the signers of the letter expressed the conviction that they could coexist in the church with those who were on their theological left.

As an outward and visible sign of this commitment, the Gang of Twelve began to meet with Progressive Episcopalians of Pittsburgh (PEP) to explore avenues of mutual cooperation. Out of this grew a coalition, organized shortly after the 142nd convention and moderated by the Rev. Nancy Chalfant Walker, then priest-in-charge of St. Stephen's, Wilkinsburg. Known as "Across the Aisle," its primary goal was to work assiduously toward rebuilding the bridges destroyed during the Duncan episcopate. It also cherished the hope that its members (it was open to anyone in the diocese who supported its mission) might actually be instrumental in

---

delivered on September 27, 2003: "The 74th [General] Convention has left us. It left the historic Faith and Order. It left mainstream Anglicanism and the ecumenical consensus of the Christian Church. It left the plain meaning of Holy Scripture. I'm not leaving. Nor are those who vote for these resolutions. Nor is the Episcopal Diocese of Pittsburgh . . . We *are* the Episcopal Church in Southwestern Pennsylvania and we intend to remain so. We are engaged in the renewal and the realignment of North American Anglicanism and we are here for the long-run to take part in this defining season, this reforming season, for, and within, the Episcopal Church."

8. Cited in Bruchi, "Breaking: Diocese of Pittsburgh," October 4, 2008

preventing the passing of the resolution at the 143rd diocesan convention, a vote that would make "realignment" a fait accompli.

The actions of the twelve conservative clergy proved personally costly. Bishop Duncan told them he felt betrayed. They were vilified by many of their colleagues who remained in Duncan's camp as traitors to the cause, and were accused of selling their birthright for a mess of pottage—the pottage in this case being the benefits of the church pension fund.[9] But the greatest cost was among congregations. Bishop Duncan had allowed for the possibility that perhaps twenty congregations—those too small to survive a rift—would collapse. He was right. And among those that survived, many were divided between clergy and people or vestry and people, or even rector and vestry. The vestry of St. Thomas, Oakmont, for example, voted six to three to remain in the Episcopal Church, and lost about a third of its communicant strength. The "realigners" formed another congregation nearby, St. John the Evangelist, under a priest who had been an associate at St. Thomas. Dissidents from Christ Church, Indiana, who did not support the vestry's decision to remain in the Episcopal Church, founded Harvest Anglican Church in Homer City, six miles away.

Bishop Duncan's bold and unambiguous actions left no doubt in the minds of the church community as to his intention to secede from the Episcopal Church and to take congregations and diocesan assets with him. In what proved to be a futile act whose purpose seemed to have been to ensure that those assets of the Episcopal Diocese of Pittsburgh would be transferred to whatever entity was created by secession, on February 2, 2007, Bishop Duncan filed papers with the Corporation Bureau of the Pennsylvania Department of State, and established and incorporated a "new"

9. Clergy who "realigned" were removed from the rolls of Episcopal clergy, and therefore no further payments could be made on their behalf into the fund. This meant that the clergy, most of whom were in early- or mid-career, would be ineligible for full benefits upon retirement, since their assets were frozen. Bishop Duncan, however, because of the length of his ministry, was fully vested in the fund, and is entitled to benefits, although certain perquisites were not forthcoming because of the CPF's policies regarding clergy who are deposed.

corporation called "Episcopal Diocese of Pittsburgh."[10] The stated purpose of his non-profit organization, of which Robert William Duncan was listed as the sole officer and signatory, was "to uphold and propagate the historic Faith and Order as set forth in the Book of Common Prayer." We believe that it is possible that this legal maneuver was initiated so that at such time as the court declared that the assets properly belonged to the Episcopal Diocese of Pittsburgh, this newly created entity could serve as a repository for those funds. The court would later put the matter to rest. In its ruling, Judge Joseph James declared, "Regardless of what name the defendants now call themselves, they are not the Episcopal Diocese of Pittsburgh of the Episcopal Church in the United States of America."[11]

While some groups, such as Across the Aisle, labored in the hopes that cooler heads would prevail and that schism could be avoided, others who supported Bishop Duncan in his quest to secede, such as the Coalition for Alignment, led by the Rev. Jonathan Millard of Ascension, Oakland, disseminated information to encourage members of the diocese to stand behind the bishop. Among these was a PowerPoint presentation created by the diocesan staff, whose message was:

> If you believe that Jesus is who he says he is;
> If you believe that the Scriptures are reliable;
> If you believe that there is such a thing as absolute truth,
> Then you must realign.

10. "Episcopal Diocese of Pittsburgh" differs considerably from the original legal name of the diocese, founded in 1865.

11. Opinion rendered by Judge Joseph James, Court of Common Pleas, October 5, 2009.

14

Bishop Duncan "Defrocked"

WHEN THE 143RD DIOCESAN convention—whose theme, ironically enough, was "A house divided against itself cannot stand"—was called to order at St. Martin's, Monroeville, on October 4, 2008, the gavel was wielded by the Rev. Jonathan Millard, rector of Church of the Ascension, who had been elected president pro tempore of the convention. Robert Duncan, listed in the materials distributed at convention as "Bishop's Commissary to the Episcopal Diocese of Pittsburgh,"[1] did not preside. The reason was that Duncan was no longer bishop of Pittsburgh, or indeed a bishop of the Episcopal Church, as the House of Bishops, at its meeting in Salt Lake City six weeks earlier, had voted to remove him from the office of bishop for having abandoned the communion of the Episcopal Church. The decision of the House came after diligent investigation and prayerful discernment. From her office in New York, the Most Rev. Katharine Jefferts Schori, presiding bishop and primate of the Episcopal Church, had been monitoring the events in the Diocese of Pittsburgh, as well as the actions and statements of its bishop at

1. A commissary is normally a priest who functions as official representative of a bishop in another diocese or province. The bishop whom Robert Duncan was purportedly representing was the Most Rev. Gregory Venables, Primate of the Southern Cone.

home and abroad. She was, so far as Robert Duncan was concerned, persona non grata in his diocese,[2] so that when on two occasions the rector of Calvary Church issued an invitation to her, in order that she might interact with the people of the diocese, permission for such visits was denied by Bishop Duncan. (The irony of such a decision was lost on no one. Duncan sought the "right" of "orthodox" bishops to minister to dissident Anglicans across diocesan and provincial boundaries, yet prevented the presiding bishop from visiting a diocese within her own province!)

On All Saints Day 2007, the eve of the 142nd convention of the Diocese of Pittsburgh, Bishop Katharine, in a public letter, issued a warning to Bishop Duncan. Citing the content of the resolutions scheduled to come before the convention, the presiding bishop informed the bishop of Pittsburgh that it was evident to her that those resolutions that he had endorsed would violate the constitutional requirement that the diocese conform to the constitution and canons of the Episcopal Church. Citing her awareness of other statements that she viewed as indicative of Duncan's intention to lead the Diocese of Pittsburgh into a position that would purportedly permit it to depart from the Episcopal Church, she asked the bishop to "recede from this direction and to lead your diocese on a new course that recognizes the interdependent and hierarchical relationship between the national Church and its dioceses and parishes." Urging him to change his position and to oppose the adoption of those resolutions, the presiding bishop continued: "If your course does not change, I shall regrettably be compelled to see that appropriate canonical steps are promptly taken to consider whether you have abandoned the Communion of this Church—by actions and substantive statements, however they may be phrased—and whether you have committed canonical offenses that warrant disciplinary action." She concluded by

2. When Bishop Jefferts Schori was elected by the House of Bishops in 2006, Bishop Duncan walked out of the House in protest. He later commented, "For the Anglican Communion worldwide, this election reveals the continuing insensitivity and disregard of the Episcopal Church for the present dynamics of our global fellowship" (Banerjee, "Woman Is Named Episcopal Leader," June 19, 2006).

reiterating an offer for "an episcopal visitor" if Duncan desired "pastoral care from another bishop."[3]The formal process of presentment, i.e., putting forward charges that could lead to deposition, does not originate in the presiding bishop's office, but rather in the diocese impacted by the bishop's ministry. Later in November 2007, the diocesan convention having run its course, a group of clergy canonically resident in the Diocese of Pittsburgh and laypersons who were adult communicants in good standing in the diocese, met in the conference room of Calvary Episcopal Church and signed a letter addressed to the Rt. Rev. Dorsey Henderson Jr., senior bishop of the review committee of TEC. The letter requested that the committee review Bishop Duncan's actions to determine if, in its opinion, they constituted grounds for deposition. An addendum of several hundred pages, containing some forty exhibits, was attached to the letter. Although Bishop Duncan declined to avail himself of the offer to be present in the House of Bishops with his attorneys to speak to the matter of whether the House should consent to his deposition, he sent instead a letter alleging that he had been denied due process.

Ultimately, on September 18, 2008, following a vote of the House of Bishops, Robert William Duncan was deposed as a bishop of the Episcopal Church by the presiding bishop. By all reports, there was no jubilation in the House. The decision whether to consent to his deposition was taken as a solemn duty and responsibility. The Rt. Rev. Gary Lillibridge, bishop of West Texas and a theological conservative, commented: "As difficult as this decision is for me and many others in our Church, it is important to realize that the decision in the House today was not based on the theological convictions of Bishop Duncan, but rather on the evidence presented regarding statements and actions concerning moves to take the Diocese of Pittsburgh out of the Episcopal Church."[4] The Rt. Rev. Paul Marshall, bishop of Bethlehem (Pennsylvania), in

3. Quoted from Nunley, "Presiding Bishop Reaches Out," October 31, 2007.

4. Conlon, "Episcopal Church Defrocks Dissident bishop," September 18, 2008.

reference to Duncan's objection that the deposition should have taken place after the diocese decided to realign, pointed out that Bishop Duncan's deposition "was not approved because of what he might do in October, but on account of what he has done heretofore. That was the only basis on which the PB, the Review Committee, or the House had any business proceeding."[5] At the end of the day, the final vote was reportedly 88 ayes, 35 nays, and four abstentions.

In his official comment on the development, the Rev. David Wilson, president of Pittsburgh's standing committee and a staunch Duncan supporter, decried the actions of the House of Bishops. Describing Duncan's ouster as "a painful moment," he added, "The leadership of the Episcopal Church *has inserted itself in a most violent manner* into the affairs and governance of our diocese. We will stand firm against any further attempts by those *outside our boundaries* to intimidate us."[6]

At the 143rd diocesan convention, the resolution first introduced at the previous year's convention, proposing "realignment" with the Province of the Southern Cone, was presented for its "second reading." It was voted upon with the following results: clergy: 121 ayes, 33 nays, three abstentions; laity: 119 ayes, 69 nays, three abstentions. When a letter from Archbishop Venables was read announcing that the Diocese of Pittsburgh had been warmly welcomed and fully recognized as a member diocese in the Province of the Southern Cone, and that Robert Duncan had been duly recognized as a bishop of that province, there was much rejoicing. Peter Frank, diocesan communications officer, welcomed this novel development: "We are deeply thankful to the Province of the Southern Cone for offering us a clear way to stay within the Anglican Communion as the necessary work of building a new province goes forward." The business of the convention was resumed. But for those who had voted against the secession, this was our cue to exit stage left. After rising for a point of personal privilege, I

5. Naughton, "Duncan Deposed," September 18, 2008.

6. Zoll, "Pittsburgh Episcopal Bishop Robert Duncan Removed," September 19, 2008, italics added.

announced that Calvary's delegation and others would be leaving the convention immediately, lest our continued presence be construed as tacit approval of what had taken place.

As we made our exit, we took no small comfort in the assurance provided in a communication from the presiding bishop: "We will work with remaining Episcopalians in Pittsburgh to provide support as they reorganize the Diocese and call a bishop to provide episcopal ministry. The people of the Episcopal Church hold all concerned in our prayers—for healing and comfort in time of distress, and for discernment as they seek their way in the future."[7]

---

7. Schjoneberg, "Pittsburgh Votes to Leave Episcopal Church, October 4, 2008.

15

Lis litem generat
(One Lawsuit Begets Another)

THE "REALIGNMENT" ENGINEERED BY Robert Duncan proceeded almost according to plan. There were sufficient numbers of clergy and people who believed that his theological and ecclesiological arguments for secession warranted their support. They believed themselves to be faithful and orthodox Anglicans untainted by the secular humanism that had, in their view, compromised the mission and ministry of the Episcopal Church. Duncan's followers, seen as persecuted pilgrims, were granted temporary asylum by a province of the Anglican Communion. It would only be a matter of time before an autonomous provincialesque structure would be formed (ACNA) and a campaign would be launched (to date an unsuccessful one) for full recognition in the Anglican Communion. But there remained the matter of the fiscal health of the new enterprise. Financial support from parishes (both former Episcopal congregations in the Diocese of Pittsburgh and "adopted" congregations beyond diocesan boundaries) would be forthcoming, but those funds would not come close to the war chest needed for Duncan's initiatives for his new church organization. The court's 2005 stipulation, to which Duncan had agreed, made it abundantly clear that he and his new church could not tap the resources of the Episcopal Diocese of Pittsburgh for this or any other purpose, but Duncan, on the other side of "realignment," adopted new strategies in an attempt to convince the courts that he was now somehow entitled to those funds.

ADDITIONAL MOTION BEFORE
THE COURT OF COMMON PLEAS

The first such attempt took place in January 2009,[1] when Duncan's attorneys filed a "Motion to restore and preserve status quo and preclude interference with diocesan property." The first two sentences of the motion speak to the ways that occurrences were characterized in order to convince the court of its merit:

> *Defendant Episcopal Diocese of Pittsburgh* completed its withdrawal from the Protestant Episcopal Church in the United States of America otherwise known as the Episcopal Church ("TEC"). Plaintiffs and a *newly-created diocese* aligned with TEC (*the "new Diocese"*) have asserted that this withdrawal is invalid and therefore Defendants have violated the October 15, 2005 Stipulation and Order. (italics added)

Note that the diocese is here referred to as "defendant," although it had not been named as defendant by plaintiffs or recognized as such by the court. Moreover, having admitted to "withdrawal" from the Episcopal Church, Duncan further alleges in the motion that his organization, owing to the majority vote at the 2007 and 2008 conventions to both remove the accession clause[2] and to realign, constituted the continuing diocese. Duncan also purported the validity of his organization on the grounds that it "continued

---

1. An amended version of the motion was filed in March 2009, which included additional information having to do with the financial hardships of defendants and other matters.

2. The diocesan conventions in 2003 and 2004 amended Article 1 of the diocesan Constitution in an attempt to qualify the diocesan accession to TEC's Constitution and Canons. The specious argument was that a diocese, once having agreed to accession, could decide to terminate such an agreement.

to have that name" (i.e., Episcopal Diocese of Pittsburgh),[3] while the motion refers to the bona fide Episcopal Diocese as the "new diocese."

The motion also alleged that the plaintiffs "attempted to assume control of the Property,"[4] an illogical assertion in light of the fact that the defendants had agreed to the stipulation that provided that the diocese continuing in the Episcopal Church would retain ownership of the property in the event that a separation took place.

On October 6, 2009, Judge Joseph James of the Court of Common Pleas in Allegheny County ruled that the existing court-approved agreement is "clear and unambiguous" in requiring that diocesan property must remain with a diocese that is part of the Episcopal Church of the United States.

The judge further opined that the former diocesan leaders are "in violation [of that agreement] and cannot continue to be the trustee" of the property. "The property is to be held or administered by the Episcopal Diocese of Pittsburgh of the Episcopal Church of the United States," Judge James wrote. In making its case, the continuing diocese argued, "After all the testimony, evidence, arguments and briefs [the defendants] cannot plausibly explain how they can hold property that under the Stipulation is to be held by the 'Episcopal Diocese of Pittsburgh of the Episcopal Church of the United States of America' when they are no longer part of the 'Episcopal Church of the United States.'" The judge added: "Regardless of what name the defendants now call themselves, they are not the Episcopal Diocese of Pittsburgh of the

3. This, of course, was a short-lived claim, since the secessionists, meeting in convention after their "withdrawal" from the Episcopal Church, later formed an entity known as the Anglican Diocese of Pittsburgh.

4. This was a reference to the fact that on November 20, 2008, Andrew Roman, chancellor of the diocese, sent a letter to Morgan Stanley, manager of investment accounts for the diocese, and instructed them that, in light of the actions of the recent diocesan convention in which Bishop Duncan and his officers had separated themselves from the Episcopal Church, said officers were no longer authorized to control or have any access to said accounts. Morgan Stanley decided that it would not allow any distributions from the accounts until it received a court order that would clarify which entity was the legitimate successor to their original clients.

Episcopal Church of the United States of America." The decision also made provision for the court to "enter an appropriate order for the orderly transition of possession, custody and control over said property."

APPEAL TO THE COMMONWEALTH
COURT OF PENNSYLVANIA

The defendants appealed the ruling of the Court of Common Pleas by arguing their case before the Commonwealth Court of Pennsylvania on November 9, 2010.[5] The appeal alleged, inter alia, that the lower court violated appellants' due process rights by denying them a full and fair opportunity to litigate the validity dispute (i.e., whether their withdrawal from the Episcopal Church was valid, and if so, that it entitled them to the assets of the Episcopal Diocese) and that the lower court erred by not dismissing Calvary's petition for enforcement of the stipulation.

The Commonwealth Court, in its opinion handed down on February 2, 2011, upheld the opinion of the Court of Common Pleas. It stated that it "agrees with the trial court that the Stipulation's meaning is clear, and we do not believe the Stipulation is reasonably susceptible to the interpretation proffered by the Anglican Diocese." The decision went on to say that the language of the stipulation is clear, and that therefore the party entitled to the property in question was "the Episcopal Diocese of Pittsburgh that remained affiliated with TEC U.S.A."

---

5. It should be noted that, by this time, the (national) Episcopal Church had become a party to the ongoing action, and was therefore among the appellees in the case. David Booth Beers, the presiding bishop's chancellor, was among the attorneys presenting arguments in support of Calvary's and the continuing diocese's position.

PETITION FOR ALLOWANCE OF APPEAL
TO THE SUPREME COURT OF PENNSYLVANIA

Robert Duncan et al., decided to attempt to take their case to the Supreme Court of Pennsylvania. That court's standards make it clear that an appeal before it is not a matter of right, but of sound judicial discretion, and appeals are allowed only under special circumstances, including: a) a case in which there is conflict between opinions rendered by intermediate appellate courts; b) an issue involving the constitutionality of a statute of the Commonwealth; c) egregious departure from accepted judicial practices or abuse of discretion on the part of the intermediate appellate courts.

In their petition, filed in March 2011, the appellants presented various arguments that, in one form or another, they had brought before the lower courts regarding the validity of the withdrawal of Duncan et al. from the Episcopal Church. They objected to the presence of representatives from TEC on the grounds that they had no authority to speak on the church's behalf. In addition, they argued that "the Commonwealth Court's decision contravenes controlling Pennsylvania Supreme Court law and the Commonwealth Court's own process regarding due process," observing that they were not given notice and opportunity for hearing at such time as they were deprived of access to the assets of the diocese. This allegation, of course, ignores the fact that they had already signed the stipulation that made it clear that, in the event of realignment or removal, the real and personal property of the diocese would not be available to them.

The Supreme Court of Pennsylvania, on October 17, 2011, issued an order stating "the Petition of Allowance of Appeal is hereby denied." This meant that the Supreme Court would not hear the case, and therefore, since for a variety of reasons there was little likelihood that the matter would be taken to the United States Supreme Court, that an important phase of the eight-year legal struggle to preserve the integrity of the Episcopal Diocese of Pittsburgh and to preserve its assets had come to an end.

Afterword
What, How, and Why?

WHAT?

WE HAVE ATTEMPTED TO show in these pages that the events that transpired in the Diocese of Pittsburgh, however unprecedented, however bizarre, during the roughly ten-year period between the election of Gene Robinson as bishop of New Hampshire and the resolution of the court case filed by Calvary Church, Pittsburgh against Robert Duncan et al., were, when all was said and done, a predictable series of events emerging from the realities of a rapidly changing global Anglicanism. The Anglican Communion, it must be remembered, is a historic outgrowth of the British Empire, on which, famously, the sun was said never to set. The cross followed the Union Jack "o'er every continent and island,"[1] and in one fell swoop colonizers and missionaries made British subjects and Anglicans of virtually all with whom they came into contact. But as the former colonies gained their independence and indigenous

---

1. From a verse in "The Day Thou Gavest, Lord, Is Ended" (Episcopal Church, *Hymnal 1982*, 24). A hymn appointed for evening, it is often understood as an allusion to the continuity and permanence of the Anglican Communion, if not the Empire: "As o'er each continent and island the dawn leads on another day / The voice of prayer is never silent, nor dies the strain of praise away" (v. 3).

presidents and prime ministers replaced British viceroys and governors-general, so too did the church raise up local clergy and lay leaders of large, vibrant churches who in the fullness of time far outnumbered the comparatively puny communities that in a previous age had "sent heralds forth to bear the message glorious."

But newly minted Anglicans in the Global South were not simply overseas replicas of the missionaries who had brought them the faith, since that faith developed and was nurtured in a radically different cultural context. This led to different theological understandings of several issues, most notably those having to do with human sexuality in general and homosexuality in particular. The more liberal view, *in nuce*, held by most "Northern" Anglicans, often frames homosexuality in a discourse of civil rights and social progress, and argues that gays and lesbians, like racial minorities and women, should be fully recognized and accepted in church and society. Not being biblical literalists, liberals offer hermeneutical explanations for those Scripture passages that seem to condemn homosexuality. The conservative view, on the other hand, begins with the same passages of Scripture and regards them as eternal and immutable truths, not subject to interpretation in light of contemporary mores. Moreover, failure to accept such teaching is seen as tantamount to questioning the authority of Holy Scripture.

Hassett observes that the predominance of tolerance for gays and lesbians in the national Episcopal Church, beginning in the early 1990s, "made conservative Episcopalians feel increasingly oppressed and embattled." As a result, she adds, "they began looking for help from the Anglican world beyond the Episcopal Church, building a network of relationships and a common agenda with Southern Anglican leaders." But while the sexuality issue was the cause célèbre, Southern conservatives were also motivated by such issues as anger at the Episcopal Church,[2] concerns about

2. Much of the anger was engendered by insensitive and derogatory statements by Episcopalians, notably the Rt. Rev. John (Jack) Spong, bishop of Newark, who asserted that African Christians were "superstitious, fundamentalist Christians" who are a short step from animism and embrace a "very superstitious kind of Christianity [and have] yet to face the intellectual revolution of Copernicus and Einstein." Kirkpatrick observed that Spong succeeded

Western morality, and cultural dominance and imperialism.[3] The Southern Anglicans were encouraged and pleased to offer "help" in the form of providing jurisdiction, or spiritual oversight—in effect a spiritual home—and episcopal acts (such as Confirmation and ordination)[4] for those Northern Anglicans who did not wish to be subject to the ministrations of bishops who did not share their "orthodoxy."[5]

Kirkpatrick has argued that the conservatives' understanding of both Scripture and the nature of the church is seriously flawed, and adds that "the traditionalists who are appealing to the Anglican tradition at best are highly selective in how they define that tradition and at worst are guilty of misreading and distorting it."[6] He observes, for example, that the Anglican tradition has always accepted as self-evident the cultural and contextual writing and interpretation of the Bible, and he criticizes the conservatives' redefinition of dioceses as "aggregates of congregations that have a like mind on certain issues" as contrary to the way that dioceses have been understood historically within Anglicanism.[7]

I cite this brief history in order that we may better understand the crucible in which I believe Bishop Duncan's theology was forged. In my view, his understanding of biblical theology and ecclesiology creates constraints that severely limit the scope of his utterances. Kirkpatrick suggests that, like many conservatives, Duncan believes "that if the Church fails to hold onto *some* moral

---

in "personifying the arrogance and cultural captivity of the American liberals" (see Kirkpatrick, *Episcopal Church in Crisis*, 4–5).

3. The election of Gene Robinson was described as an "imperialistic act"—an example of Western culture imposing its mores on the rest of the world—by no fewer than three archbishops: Nigeria, Uganda, and Southeast Asia (Lewis, *Church for the Future*, 103).

4. All Anglican churches are "episcopal," that is, they depend upon the ministrations of bishops for their ongoing functioning. Only bishops can confirm laypersons to exercise a lay apostolate, and only bishops can ordain bishops, priests, and deacons, to ensure the continuance of the ordained ministry.

5. Hassett, *Anglican Communion in Crisis*, 4ff.

6. Kirkpatrick, *Episcopal Church in Crisis*, 165.

7. Ibid., 168.

absolutes, moral anarchy and secular relativism will be loosed upon the world."[8] Such views may lead to the use of hyperbole, such as suggesting that the network is akin to the Confessing Church under Nazi persecution, or praying that conservatives be slated for a "red martyrdom."[9] In our own context, then, we understand why Bishop Duncan would resort to an attempt to evict "offending" parishes from the diocese. In the first place, we were thought to be guilty of unbiblical behavior (suing fellow Christians in court); and secondly, we had disobeyed a godly admonition (to cease and desist our actions) an offense against the bishop and therefore of church order. In dealing with the situation, Duncan stated things in black and white, rather than in shades of gray.

In an interview with the *Post-Gazette* several months after the consecration of Gene Robinson, Duncan defined revisionism as changing what had been received (or "once delivered to the saints") and equated it with heresy or the abandonment of the truth. Asked if it was worth breaking up the Episcopal Church, and potentially the Anglican Communion, in pursuit of that truth, Duncan replied, "You can't have unity without truth and you can't have truth without unity."[10] This suggests to me that Duncan's ecclesiology, his understanding of the nature of the church, is so predicated on what he perceives as absolute truth that anything that allegedly stands in the way of that truth is dispensable, even (or we might even say, especially) existing church structures.

Bishop Duncan's strong reaction against our suit and his arguments in the suit suggest that he believed that the courts had no jurisdiction over church matters. He explained that he only entered into the legal fray because, having been sued, he felt it his

8. Ibid., 169.

9. In a statement issued by Bishop Duncan on the occasion of the organization of the Common Cause Partnership of bishops, September 28, 2007, he said: "My prayer for us who have gathered here is that . . . we will be such a threat to the present order that we will be found worth killing, if only Columba's white martyrdom, but, if it be so, let it be the red martyrdom" (Schjonberg, "Common Cause Bishops").

10. Keough, "Who Is Doing the Dividing?"

responsibility to mount, in his own words, "a vigorous defense."[11] In addition to challenging the stipulation in the courts, Bishop Duncan put his energies into trying to persuade Calvary and St. Stephen's, Wilkinsburg to drop the suit entirely. This was done, as we have observed, by threatening to expel our parishes from the diocese. We were also publicly challenged at clergy conferences and diocesan conventions, openly blamed for diocesan fiscal shortfalls, and continually urged by many of our fellow clergy to withdraw the suit. Finally Diane Shepherd, the rector of St. Stephen's, and I were invited to a series of luncheons with Geoff Chapman (of "memo" fame), the rector of St. Stephen's, Sewickley, and Jonathan Millard, the rector of Ascension, Oakland, at which those clergy, acting at the bishop's behest, urged us to drop the lawsuit forthwith.

It was under such constraints that we labored in the period of uncertainty and upheaval during the days of the most recent unpleasantness in the Diocese of Pittsburgh.

HOW?

How have we approached the task of rebuilding as a diocese? The first order of business, arguably, was to examine the status of our congregations. The courts' ruling on the appeals notwithstanding, we were still not out of the woods. The stipulation had specified two distinct types of property. There were properties, real and personal, belonging to the diocese in its own right, such as its endowments, investments, and savings accounts, equipment, etc. There were also properties belonging to (or more specifically, held in

11. "In the sad matter of the civil suit brought by two of our parishes, and now re-entered by one of them, the Standing Committee has concurred in my decision to respond with a vigorous defense. The matters in play are theological and ecclesiastical. They have nothing to do with the property of the diocese. The property of the Episcopal Diocese of Pittsburgh will continue to be held and administered for the beneficial use of the parishes and institutions of the diocese. It is our continuing commitment to protect the interest the diocese has in its property—indeed to protect all that it is steward over—against any who would attempt to usurp that role, either from below (minority parishes) or above (national church)" (Duncan, "Pastoral Letter," January 30, 2007).

trust by) individual parishes and congregations.[12] While, by strict interpretation of the Dennis Canon, the congregations who had seceded were bound to "turn over the keys" of any parish property that they continued to use under the auspices of the ACNA diocese, the court encouraged amicable arrangements regarding the property, such as retention of property upon payment (at "fair market value") to the Episcopal Diocese. It was expected that this would be done on a case-by-case basis, and court approval was required for each such arrangement.

St. Philip's in Moon Township was the first to step up to the plate, in February 2011. Upon negotiating a price for their property, the parish leadership informed now Archbishop Duncan of their decision to withdraw from ACNA to become an independent church. The rector, Eric Taylor, commented that the religious affiliation of the church was less important than their "commitment to the people of Moon Township [and] to the kids and families we care about, to tell them about Jesus."[13] Duncan decried the decision and alleged that the Episcopal Diocese's actions in the matter were "specifically designed to hurt both the local [ACNA] diocese and the North American province." Since the arrangement required the parish to sever ties with ACNA, Duncan charged that the Episcopal diocese had deprived St. Philip's of its First Amendment right to freedom of religion, and urged the court to strike down the severance requirement.

While Duncan may well have been concerned about a perceived violation of constitutional rights, the fact that St. Philip's separation from ACNA would deprive his new diocese of one of its largest assessments, amounting to tens of thousands of dollars annually, presented its own concerns. Moreover, he doubtless calculated the cost to his operation if the St. Philip's model were replicated throughout his diocese. It was not surprising, therefore, that Duncan, in an action that contravened ACNA's constitution and canons, issued an order barring congregations in the ACNA

12. There were some exceptions to this "rule." In some cases, the property of local congregations was deeded to the diocese.

13. Rodgers, "Moon Church to Vote on Settlement," February 1, 2011.

diocese from negotiating directly with the Episcopal diocese, and that going forward, any arrangement would have to be approved by the ACNA diocesan standing committee.[14]

Three days after the agreement with St. Philip's was announced, another congregation, Somerset Anglican Fellowship,[15] also entered into an arrangement with the diocese. Within a week of the signing of that agreement, the Rt. Rev. Kenneth Price, interim bishop of the Episcopal diocese, holding up both recent events as models of virtually seamless negotiations, sent a letter and "pastoral direction" to all forty-one ACNA congregations. In it, he invited those congregations to enter into negotiations with the diocese in order that they too could achieve an orderly transference of property. Bishop Price encouraged "amicable agreements" in the hopes that they would render unnecessary "the controversy of litigation" and so that the congregations could instead "focus more intently on their respective Gospel ministries." His letter also contained a warning that failure to participate in the life of the diocese for two years or more could result in their being designated as "transitional parishes," which would mean that all parish property would become vested in the board of trustees of the Episcopal diocese if that was not already the case. The congregations were given a month after the date of the letter to notify the bishop of their intentions.

Despite Bishop Price's overture, which was widely reported in the press,[16] no additional arrangements between an ACNA

14. "ACNA Bishop Bob Duncan issued a pastoral directive forbidding any ACNA clergy and vestry members from speaking to the Episcopal Diocese about property issues without his permission. The ACNA Constitution and Canons say that every ACNA congregation is free to manage and dispose of their property without interference from the denomination. Their Constitution and Canons also state that ACNA 'respects' situations where the congregation may not hold title to their property" (Gems, "Pastoral Direction in Pittsburgh," February 18, 2011).

15. Whereas St. Philip's agreed to keep its property and make payments to the Episcopal Diocese, the Somerset congregation agreed to surrender its property in order to affiliate with any religious body of its choosing.

16. See, e.g., Robbins, "Property Next Matter," April 4, 2011, which reported that both the ACNA parishes and the Episcopal diocese were ready to

congregation and the Episcopal diocese have been reported to date.[17] The people of the diocese are unaware of whether that is because no offers have been made or because negotiations have been unsuccessful. But we know from Dr. Joan Gundersen, property administrator for the diocese, that some congregations that had voted to affiliate with ACNA have come back to the Episcopal fold. Other ACNA congregations later discovered they could no longer maintain their properties or had lost significant membership, or have abandoned their original buildings and sought another church home. (Of these, some buildings have been restored to use as Episcopal congregations, and others have been rented to church and non-church groups.) Dr. Gundersen's most recent accounting is that there are eight "properties still occupied by ACNA congregations" and fifteen "properties where the deed runs in the name of the parish but in which the Episcopal Diocese has a trust interest."[18]

Special mention should be made of Trinity Cathedral, which, under an agreement entered into before the schism, purported that as a "house of prayer for all people" it could be home to both the Episcopal and ACNA dioceses. But that plan proved short-lived. In December 2011, the chapter[19] voted to affirm Trinity's Charter of Incorporation, which states that it exists "for the support and maintenance of a cathedral church for the public worship

---

negotiate.

17. There has been one exception. In October 2012, the diocese entered into an agreement with Shepherd's Heart, a ministry to the homeless, the addicted, and other marginalized communities. To enable it to carry out this unique ministry, the diocese "left the value of its current equity in the property in place as an investment [in Shepherd's Heart] for as long as its outreach to the homeless continues" (Episcopal Diocese of Pittsburgh, "Agreement Affirms Commitment").

18. Gundersen, "State of the Property," June 17, 2013.

19. The chapter is, in effect, the vestry of a cathedral. In the Diocese of Pittsburgh, it includes members elected by the diocesan convention in addition to those elected by the congregation. Under the cathedral's short-lived plan to be home to both dioceses, the number of Episcopalians and the number of ACNA parishioners was specified, so as to achieve equal representation of each group.

of Almighty God *according to the faith, doctrine and discipline of the Protestant Episcopal Church in the United States of America,"* and further states that it *"acknowledges religious allegiance to the Protestant Episcopal Church in the United States of America and that portion of the same known as the Diocese of Pittsburgh and will be subject to and governed by the laws, rules and regulations of the same as set forth in the constitutions and canons of said Church and said Diocese."* Archbishop Duncan, not surprisingly, denounced the decision, saying that the chapter had "chosen to embrace exclusivity, rather than inclusivity."[20]

But these data do not tell the human story. While Duncan often boasted that a majority of the parishes of the diocese had voted to realign (and indeed tried to use this fact as justification for claiming a right to the diocesan assets), there was, nevertheless, much dissension in the ranks. Parishioners who did not support their vestries' decisions to secede found themselves bereft of a church home, which led them in some instances to affiliate with existing congregations. Likewise, as we have pointed out, dissidents who were not in favor of their vestries' decisions to remain in the Episcopal Church founded breakaway congregations. Some such displaced persons found refuge in other denominations, while others, disillusioned, ended up not going to church at all. Still other congregations, hastily "planted" to help ensure the success of the realignment plan, collapsed under the strain.[21] Members of some families suffered the pain of finding themselves on both sides of the theological divide. In an atmosphere in which there was often no tolerance for difference of opinion, there were new divisions among Episcopalians who "learned" during the struggle that those on the other side of the issues could no longer remain their friends. Ann Rodgers, religion editor of the *Pittsburgh Post-Gazette*, commented, "There is sadness over broken relationships

20. "Trinity Cathedral Reverts Back," December 16, 2011.

21. It should be noted that some parishes actually experienced an increase in membership during this period. These were, by and large moderate or progressive congregations, such as Calvary, Redeemer and St. Stephen's, Wilkinsburg, that did not insist that its members choose sides on the issues that led to schism, but rather left such matters to individual conscience.

and anger over property litigation." She added, optimistically, however, "But relations are more amicable than in most other fractured dioceses."[22]

The second half of Ms. Rodgers' statement is, in my view, attributable to the fact that the litigation that virtually consumed the life of the Diocese of Pittsburgh for nearly a decade was not the cause of the acrimony and distrust that were all too evident in diocesan life. Rather, those feelings predated the litigation. Those of us who took legal action did not embrace the belief that its primary purpose was to heal the diocese (although that action was instrumental in the bringing about of healing over time). Its purpose, rather, was to uphold the rule of law and to prevent the then diocesan leadership from leaving the Episcopal Church with assets that rightfully belonged to the Church.

We were fortunate that the new diocesan leadership knew intuitively that they would need to be just as intentional in gathering the flock together as the old regime had been in its efforts that eventually divided it. This process began with two interim bishops, Robert Johnson and Kenneth Price, who set about the business of making the diocese whole again. They convinced its members that, in the words of an old Negro spiritual, there was "plenty good room in my Father's Kingdom"; that is, there was, in keeping with the spirit of the "broad tent" of Anglicanism, room for disagreement and differences of opinion. Those who embraced divergent opinions, even on the major issues that have threatened the unity of the Church, are not to be shunned or maligned, but, in the spirit of *ubuntu*,[23] loved and accepted. With each diocesan gathering, we learned to listen to one another, to trust one another, and even to

---

22. Rodgers, "Churches Attempt to Heal after Split," July 26, 2009.

23. "As defined by Archbishop Desmond Tutu, a person with *Ubuntu* is open and available to others, affirming of others, does not feel threatened that others are able and good, for he or she has a proper self-assurance that comes from knowing that he or she belongs in a greater whole and is diminished when others are humiliated or diminished, when others are tortured or oppressed. The African spiritual principle of *Ubuntu* offers believers a new and radical way of reading the Gospel and understanding the heart of the Christian faith" (Battle, *Ubuntu*, 40–41).

laugh with one another—behavior that had been conspicuous by its absence for well over a decade.

The healing process continued with the election of the eighth bishop of Pittsburgh. It was universally recognized that that election was an important one, as it would, at a crucial juncture in the life of the diocese, set the tone for its future. On the sixth ballot of a hard-fought election, which became a virtual choice between a liberal candidate and a conservative one, the conservative emerged as the choice of the clergy and people. But Dorsey McConnell has proved to be a conservative centrist, a listener and reconciler. His first major decision as bishop centered around the issue of human sexuality, and more particularly, whether he, as the ordinary, would allow clergy in the Diocese of Pittsburgh to use the rite approved at the 2012 General Convention for the blessing of same-sex unions. He listened to the diocese for an entire year in an effort to identify a consensus fidelium. In his pastoral letter to the diocese on November 25, 2013, Bishop McConnell expressed his hope that in all things the clergy and people of the diocese "would find a way to hold onto one other in Christ, setting an example for the world by our love." He went on to express, too, that "unity in diversity has been in the forefront of expressed values since the earliest days of rebuilding that took place in this diocese after 2008," and that despite differences and disagreement, "by being united in greater measure by our faith expressed in the Creeds [and] by the authority of Scripture, tradition and reason in our common life" we could forge a "commitment both to the order of the Episcopal Church and the fellowship of the Anglican Communion." Out of this reasoning came the bishop's decision to provide for a "local option" under which each pastor, in deciding whether to use the rite, may "minister pastorally according to his or her commitment and conscience, while putting none under constraint or duress."[24]

While his ruling on the use of the rite for same-sex blessings is not the only decision of importance Bishop McConnell has made since his consecration, we hold it up here because its language offers a stark contrast to the uncompromising language

24. McConnell, "Pastoral Letter."

of his predecessor years earlier, when another matter having to do with human sexuality was cited as the ostensible reason for a decision to separate from the Episcopal Church. It is clear that a new day has dawned on the Episcopal Diocese of Pittsburgh.

WHY?

Calvary's DNA

At least one question remains to be answered: Why did Calvary Church rise to the challenge and attempt to preserve the integrity of the Episcopal Diocese of Pittsburgh? And what accounted for the fact that it proved to be such a formidable foe, able to stand up against its bishop? The answer begins, I think, with the history and tradition of the parish. Calvary Church, East Liberty, came into being in 1855, ten years before the Episcopal Diocese of Pittsburgh. Early records of the parish show that one of its founding vestrymen was Senator (also known as General) William Wilkins. A distinguished jurist, he had served in both houses of Congress, and was Secretary of War under President Tyler. But it was his wife, Matilda Dallas Wilkins (1789–1891), daughter of Alexander James Dallas, a prominent Philadelphia attorney who was Secretary of the Treasury under President Madison, who is affectionately regarded as Calvary's Mother Foundress.

Pittsburgh at that time was part of the Diocese of Pennsylvania, when that diocese was comprised of the entire state.[25] On an occasion when the bishop, Alonzo Potter, made a visitation to Trinity Church, Pittsburgh, Mrs. Wilkins requested a brief audience with her father-in-God, during which she asked that, inasmuch as it was a long and arduous carriage ride to Trinity from the city's East End, the bishop might consider establishing a parish there.

25. There are now five dioceses in the state: Pennsylvania, in the eastern part of the state, centered around its see city, Philadelphia; Bethlehem, in the northeast; Central Pennsylvania, whose see city is Harrisburg; Pittsburgh, made up of counties in southwest Pennsylvania; and Northwestern Pennsylvania (formerly named for its see city, Ere), which was part of the Diocese of Pittsburgh until 1910.

The bishop flatly refused, and returned to Philadelphia. Matilda Wilkins, undaunted, drove back to "Homewood," the Wilkins' baronial estate in the East End[26] (after which the surrounding neighborhood is now named), and called together several of her closest friends. They met in Louis Castner's drug store in East Liberty[27] and proceeded to found Calvary Church despite the bishop's objections! Some have argued that there has long been something in Calvary's DNA that has enabled her to challenge episcopal leadership for good cause.

But there was an even more important aspect of Calvary's DNA, which became apparent in another event early in Calvary's history. It demonstrated that Calvary possessed a strong sense of commitment to the Episcopal Church and a recognition of the authority of the office of bishop. Calvary's third rector, the Rev. Joseph D. Wilson, served the parish from 1867 until 1874. Although his rectorship was marked by exponential growth both in church and Sunday school membership, he resigned in order to enter the ministry of the Reformed Episcopal Church.[28] According to Calvary's *Centennial History*, his decision was the cause of great parish upheaval. As the rector was "universally beloved, . . . many showed their affection by urging that he should remain and the Parish

26. It is described in the parish history as "a mansion, one of the finest west of the Alleghenies," where personages such as Generals Lafayette and Taylor, and Daniel Webster and Henry Clay had been entertained.

27. Alzo, *Pittsburgh's Immigrants*, 48. The parish centennial history, however, records that the meeting took place in the German Lutheran Church in East Liberty.

28. The Reformed Episcopal Church was founded in 1873 by Bishop George Cummins of Kentucky. The REC was concerned that the Catholic influence of the Oxford Movement had threatened to deprive the Episcopal Church of its Protestant, Evangelical, Reformed, and Confessional principles. It is interesting to note that the REC became, in 2009, a founding member of the Anglican Church of North America, of which Robert Duncan is archbishop! Bishop Kerfoot of Pittsburgh described Wilson's defection to the REC as the "distressed act of a man frightened in a nightmare" and Wilson himself as "guilty of great lack of memory, of history, of theology of logic and of love" (in Guelzo, *For the Union of Evangelical Christendom, passim*).

transferred to the newly formed organization." But not withstanding such affection for their pastor,

> the Vestry acted promptly and positively in their allegiance to the [Episcopal] Church and the parish by at once surrendering the Parish into the spiritual charge of the Bishop [John B. Kerfoot] and refusing to violate its charter and its own good faith by retaining Mr. Wilson in his new relations, as they were formally petitioned to do by part of the congregation.[29]

In other words, Calvary's vestry resolutely refused to allow the parish to affiliate with the breakaway sect or to continue to recognize the Rev. Mr. Wilson as its rector. It can be seen that the very principles that would motivate the vestry of Calvary to take legal action against the bishop in 2003 were virtually identical to the principles that led the vestry in 1874 to ally with the bishop and to place the congregation under his spiritual authority. In neither case was sentiment or politics in play; the issue in both situations was the preservation of the integrity of the Episcopal Church. While it would be a hundred years before these principles would be codified in the Dennis Canon, the basic premises of that legislation were at work in the minds of her wardens and vestrymen when Calvary Parish was less than twenty-five years old.

Another factor in the composition of the parish, from the time of its founding until the present, has been that among its members have been the "movers and shakers" of Pittsburgh, people, by and large, of not inconsequential means. Leaders in industry, commerce, politics, education, medicine, and law were among the first vestrymen of the parish who were influential in laying the foundation of a congregation that soon became known for its missionary zeal[30] and its unstinting munificence throughout the

---

29. Calvary Episcopal Church, *Centennial History*, 9, italics added. Rev. Wilson started a REC congregation nearby, and it lasted for about two years!

30. Calvary was the mother church of number of missions, which became flourishing parishes in their own right. They include such churches as St. Stephen's in Wilkinsburg, St. Michael's-of-the-Valley in Ligonier, Fox Chapel Episcopal Church in Fox Chapel, and Church of the Ascension in Oakland. In a unique gesture of evangelism, Calvary would become, in 1921, the first

city.[31] What is more, their counterparts in every generation have honored and continued that tradition. We mention this because the combination of expertise and wealth was essential, both in the unforeseen circumstances of the founding of the parish, as well as in the unforeseen circumstances of 2003, when the parish filed suit against the seventh bishop of Pittsburgh.

Justice, it has been said, is slow and expensive. The annals of jurisprudence are replete with stories of hapless litigants, armed only with the truth, who were unable to spend equivalently to their adversaries or who did not have the time at their disposal to pursue their plaint. Calvary is fortunate in that parish leaders had seen fit, early in the twentieth century, to establish at Calvary a substantial endowment whose income would be used, at the discretion of the vestry, for good works. It is to the vestry's credit that in 2003 it voted to pledge a portion of that income for the purpose of initiating and sustaining legal action whose purpose was to preserve the assets of the Episcopal Diocese of Pittsburgh.

Through the stipulation resolving the litigation, Calvary was essentially reimbursed for all expenses that it incurred, from an escrow account that had been created early in the litigation, to hold Calvary's payment of the diocesan assessment.[32]

Justice and the Rule of Law

Justice, as I have observed elsewhere,[33] means, at one level, doing what is right, just, and pleasing in God's sight. But at a deeper (and

church in the U. S. to broadcast a service of worship on the radio.

31. Early in the ministry of Calvary's fourth rector, Boyd Vincent (1874–1889), "a Rector's Aid Society was formed . . . gifts were given to charity, and work among the sick and poor of the Parish was accomplished, as well as contributions to missions . . . By his efforts the Parish was brought into the active, efficient, well-organized condition which has ever since marked its history, making it 'a Parish known throughout the Church' for its good works" (Calvary Episcopal Church, *Centennial History*, 11).

32. In addition, as has been noted, Calvary's costs were offset to a small degree by donations from individuals and parishes.

33. Lewis, *Christian Social Witness*, 5ff.

biblical) level, it conveys a sense of advocacy—of taking up the cause of groups who have been abused and mistreated by those in power. While we usually think that groups in need of such advocacy are the poor, or those belonging, perhaps, to racial and sexual minorities, in this case we deemed that those in need of justice, and could benefit from our advocacy, our social witness, were the members of the Episcopal Church in the Diocese of Pittsburgh. Our legal action, we maintain, was an outward and visible sign of the response to the question in the Baptismal Covenant: "Will you strive for justice and peace among all people, and respect the dignity of every human being?" (*Book of Common Prayer*, 305).

To those who would maintain that suing a bishop of the church in open court is an unorthodox way of seeking justice, we would respond with the words of a hymn: "New occasions teach new duties / Time makes ancient good uncouth."[34] The demands of our baptismal covenant must be reexamined in light of the exigencies of a changing society. All of us must discern the ways in which we may render social witness, thereby exercising our respective ministries in the name of him who came "not to be served but to serve, and to give his life as a ransom for many" (Matt 20:38).

34. James Russell Lowell, "Once to Every Man and Nation," in Episcopal Church, *Hymnal 1940*, 519.

Bibliography

Alzo, Linda. *Pittsburgh's Immigrants*. Charleston: Acadia, 2006.

Anglican Diocese of Pittsburgh. "Constitution & Canons." Online: http://s3. amazonaws.com/churchplantmedia-cms/anglican_diocese_pittsburgh/ constitution-and-canons-mmt-recall-as-to-revisions-3-3-2015.pdf.

Ayres, Russell W., III. "Some Reflections on the Primates' Communiqué." *Agape* (Calvary Church newsletter), February 24, 2007.

Banerjee, Neela. "Conservative Episcopalians Warn Church That It Must Change Course or Face Split." *New York Times*, November 12, 2005. Online: http://www.nytimes.com/2005/11/12/national/12episcopal.html.

————. "Woman Is Named Episcopal Leader." *New York Times*, June 19, 2006. Online: http://www.nytimes.com/2006/06/19/us/19bishop.html.

Banse, Robert. Open letter to the Rt. Rev. Robert William Duncan. September 14, 2003.

Battle, Michael. *Ubuntu: I in You and You in Me*. New York: Seabury, 2009.

Battle, Michael, Katherine Grieb, Jay Johnson, Mark McIntosh, Catherine Roskam, Timothy Sedgwick, and Kathryn Tanner. *To Set Our Hope on Christ: A Response to the Invitation of Windsor Report*. New York: Episcopal Church Center, June 2005. Online: http://archive.episcopalchurch.org/ documents/ToSetOurHope_eng.pdf.

Bone, James. "Church begins property wrangle as schism looms Online: http:// www.thetimes.co.uk/tto/news/world/article1967641.

Bruchi, Jackie. "Breaking: Diocese of Pittsburgh Begins Process to Recall Bishop Duncan." *Stand Firm*, October 4, 2008. Online: http://www. standfirminfaith.com/?/sf/page/16722.

Calvary Episcopal Church. *Centennial History, Calvary Episcopal Church, 1855–1955*. Pittsburgh, PA: n.p., 1955.

Church of Ireland. "Irish Anglican Consultative Council (ACC) Members Comment on Recent Developments in the Anglican Communion." Press release, February 26, 2005. Online: http://ireland.anglican.org/news/346.

Conlon, Michael. "Episcopal Church Defrocks Dissident Bishop." Reuters, September 18, 2008. Online: http://www.reuters.com/article/2008/09/19/us-religion-episcopal-idUSN1840646820080919.

"Consecrations Harmful to Unity." *The Living Church*, July 15, 2001, 14 . Online: http://www.episcopalarchives.org/cgi-bin/the_living_church/TLCarticle.pl?volume=223&issue=3&article_id=17.

Cooperman, Alan. "Plan to Supplant Episcopal Church USA Is Revealed." *Washington Post*, January 14, 2004, A04. Online: http://pqasb.pqarchiver.com/washingtonpost/doc/409617691.html.

Douglas, Ian. "The Exigency of Times and Occasions: Power and Identity in the Anglican Communion Today." In *Beyond Colonial Anglicanism: The Anglican Communion in the Twenty-First Century*, edited by Ian T. Douglas and Kwok Pui-lan, 25–46. New York: Church Publishing, 2001.

Duncan, Robert William. "The Future of Anglicanism." Address for the convocation of Nashotah House, Nashotah, WI, October 25, 2006. Online: http://www.globalsouthanglican.org/index.php/blog/comments/the_future_of_anglicanism_bishop_bob_duncan.

———. "A Pastoral Letter from Bishop Robert Duncan." January 29, 2007. Posted on *Global South Anglican*, January 30, 2007. Online: http://www.globalsouthanglican.org/index.php/blog/comments/a_pastoral_letter_from_bishop_robert_duncan.———. "A Report, a Call and a Teaching for the Leadership." September 2003.

Duncan, Robert William, et al. "An Open Letter to the Concerned Primates of the Anglican Communion." July 15, 2003. Online: http://philippians-1-20.us/primo717.htm.

Episcopal Church. *The Hymnal of the Protestant Episcopal Church in the United States of America, 1940*. New York: Church Pension Fund, 1940.

———. *The Hymnal 1982*. New York: Church Hymnal Corp., 1985.

Episcopal Diocese of Pittsburgh. "Agreement Affirms Commitment to Shepherd's Heart Homeless Ministry." October 9, 2012. Online: http://www.episcopalpgh.org/agreement-affirms-commitment-to-shepherds-heart-homeless-ministry/.

""Episcopal Priest Files Suit over Property." Associated Press, October 26, 2003. Online: http://www.ocala.com/article/20031026/NEWS/210260318.

Father Jake. "For Those Who Missed It: The Chapman Memo." *Father Jake Stops the World*, March 30, 2007. Online: http://frjakestopstheworld.blogspot.com/2007/03/for-those-who-missed-it-chapman-memo.html.

Gems, Andrew. "Pastoral Direction in Pittsburgh." Gems, *The Episcopal Café*, February 18, 2011. Online: http://www.episcopalcafe.com/pastoral_direction_in_pittsburgh/.

"Groups Call for Repudiation of American Anglican Council and Network." *The Witness*, A Globe of Witnesses, January 20, 2004. Online: http://www.thewitness.org/agw/aaco12204.html.

Guelzo, Allen C. *For the Union of Evangelical Christendom: The Irony of the Reformed Episcopal Church*. University Park: Pennsylvania State University Press, 1994.

Gundersen, Joan R. "A History of the Episcopal Church in the Diocese of Pittsburgh." *Archives of the Episcopal Diocese of Pittsburgh*, March 12, 2013. Online: http://www.episcopalpgh.org/archives/resources/history/.

———. "The State of the Property." Paper presented at a meeting of the Progressive Episcopalians of Pittsburgh, Calvary Church, Pittsburgh, June 17, 2013.

Hassett, Miranda Katherine. *Anglican Communion in Crisis: How Episcopal Dissidents and Their African Allies Are Reshaping Anglicanism*. Princeton, NJ: Princeton University Press, 2007.

Hefling, Charles C. *Our Selves, Our Souls, and Bodies: Sexuality and the Household of God*. Cambridge, MA: Cowley, 1996.

Higgins, Andrew. "Episcopal Church Dissidents Seek Authority Overseas." *Wall Street Journal*, September 20, 2007. Online: http://www.wsj.com/articles/SB119023295621032668.

Keough, Diane. "Who Is Doing the Dividing?" Beliefnet, February 2004. Online: http://www.beliefnet.com/Faiths/Christianity/2004/02/Who-Is-Doing-The-Dividing.aspx.

Kirkpatrick, Frank G. *The Episcopal Church in Crisis: How Sex, the Bible, and Authority Are Dividing the Faithful*. Westport, CT: Praeger, 2008.

Lambeth Commission on Communion. "The Windsor Report." London: Anglican Communion Office, 2004.

LeBlanc, Douglas. "Windsor Report Leaves Conservative Episcopalians Hopping Mad." *Christianity Today* (web only), October 1, 2004. Online: http://www.christianitytoday.com/ct/2004/octoberweb-only/10-18-25.0.html.

Levin, Steve. "Letter Shows Rift among Episcopal Conservatives." *Pittsburgh Post-Gazette*, January 30, 2008. Online: http://www.post-gazette.com/frontpage/2008/01/30/Letter-shows-rift-among-Episcopal-conservatives.

———. "Rector Criticizes Prevailing Conservatism as 'Uncharitable . . . Misguided . . . Wrong." *Pittsburgh Post-Gazette*, February 25, 2007. Online: http://www.post-gazette.com/frontpage/2007/02/25/Rector-criticizes-church-s-prevailing-conservativism-as-uncharitable-misguided-wrong.

Lewis, Harold T. *Christian Social Witness*. Cambridge, MA: Cowley, 2001.

———. *A Church for the Future: South Africa as the Crucible for Anglicanism in a New Century*. New York: Church Publishing, 2007.

———. "Covenant, Contract and Communion: Reflections on a Post-Windsor Anglicanism." *Anglican Theological Review* 87 (2005) 601–8.

———. Letter to the Rt. Rev. Robert William Duncan. April 22, 1998.

———. *Yet with a Steady Beat: The African American Struggle for Recognition in the Episcopal Church*. Valley Forge, PA: Trinity, 1996.

Lewis, Harold T., Margaret S. Austin, Charles M. Grimstad, James F. Bauerle, and Deborah Dodds. "An Open Letter to the Bishop and Bishop

Coadjutor of Pittsburgh from the Clergy, Wardens and Vestry of Calvary Episcopal Church, Pittsburgh, Pennsylvania." June 9, 1997. Online: http://theroadtoemmaus.org/RdLb/32Ang/Epis/PghPastLtr.htm.

McConnell, Dorsey W. M. "A Pastoral Letter from Bishop McConnell." Episcopal Diocese of Pittsburgh, November 25, 2013. Online: http://www.episcopalpgh.org/a-pastoral-letter-from-bishop-mcconnell/.

Naughton, Jim. "Duncan Deposed." *The Episcopal Café*, September 18, 2008. Online: http://www.episcopalcafe.com/duncan_deposed/.

Nunley, Jan. "Presiding Bishop Reaches Out to Bishops Attempting to Withdraw Dioceses." Episcopal News Service, October 31, 2007. Online: http://archive.episcopalchurch.org/79425_91480_ENG_HTM.htm.

Orombi, Henry Luke. "Archbishop Henry Orombi of Uganda on the Primates Meeting." *Global South Anglican*, February 21, 2007. Online: http://www.globalsouthanglican.org/index.php/blog/comments/archbishop_henry_orombi_of_uganda_on_the_primates_meeting.

————. Letter to "Rectors, Clergy and Lay Leaders in Ugandan Churches in America." June 22, 2007. Online: http://babybluecafe.blogspot.com/2007/06/breaking-news-john-guernsey-to-be.html.

"PB's Choice to Preach in Belfast Doubted." *The Living Church*, February 25, 2005.

Peers, Michael. "Canada: Statement by Archbishop Michael Peers." Anglican Communion News Service, February 8, 2000. Online: http://www.anglicannews.org/news/2000/02/canada-statement-by-archbishop-michael-peers.aspx.

Pew Research Center. "Anglicanism and Global Affairs: The Windsor Report and Beyond." Transcript, October 19, 2004. Online: http://www.pewforum.org/2004/10/19/anglicanism-and-global-affairs-the-windsor-report-and-beyond/.

"Pittsburgh: Trinity Cathedral Reverts Back to Episcopal Church Diocese." *VirtueOnline*, December 16, 2011. Online: http://www.virtueonline.org/pittsburgh-trinity-cathedral-reverts-back-episcopal-church-diocese.

Progressive Episcopalians of Pittsburgh. "October 8th Letter to Primates." October 8, 2003. Online: http://progressiveepiscopalians.org/html/oct8.html.

"Primates' Meeting Communiqué." Episcopal News Service, February 24, 2005. Online: http://archive.episcopalchurch.org/3577_59050_ENG_HTM.htm.

"Primates' Meeting Communiqué." Episcopal News Service, February 19, 2007. Online: http://archive.episcopalchurch.org/3577_82571_ENG_HTM.htm.

"Primates 'Out for Blood' at Meeting." *The Living Church*, March 15, 2005. Online: https://geoconger.wordpress.com/2005/03/15/presiding-bishop-primates-%E2%80%9Cout-for-blood%E2%80%9D-at-meeting-tlc-31505/.

"Request for Alternative Primatial Oversight and Pastoral Care on Behalf of the Episcopal Diocese of Pittsburgh." November 6, 2006. Online: http://www.globalsouthanglican.org/index.php/blog/printing/full_text_of_the_request_to_the_global_south_primates_diocese_of_pittsburgh.

Robbins, Richard. "Property Next Matter for Anglican Parishes." *TribLIVE News*, April 4, 2011. Online: http://triblive.com/x/valleyindependent/news/s_730629.html.

Rodgers, Ann. "Churches Attempt to Heal after Split." *Pittsburgh Post-Gazette*, July 26, 2009. Online: http://www.post-gazette.com/local/region/2009/07/26/Churches-attempt-to-heal-after-split.

———. "Moon Church to Vote on Settlement with Episcopal Diocese." *Pittsburgh Post-Gazette*, February 1, 2011. Online: http://www.post-gazette.com/local/west/2011/02/01/Moon-church-to-vote-on-settlement-with-Episcopal-diocese.

Schjonberg, Mary Frances. "Common Cause Bishops Pledge to Seek Anglican Recognition." Episcopal News Service, September 28, 2007. Online: http://archive.episcopalchurch.org/79425_90545_ENG_HTM.htm.

———. "Pittsburgh: Parish Asks Court to Protect Diocesan Property." Episcopal News Service, December 22, 2006. Online: http://archive.episcopalchurch.org/3577_80714_ENG_HTM.htm.

———. "Pittsburgh Votes to Leave Episcopal Church, Align with Southern Cone." Episcopal News Service, October 4, 2008. Online: http://archive.episcopalchurch.org/79425_101322_ENG_HTM.htm.

"A Statement by the Primates of the Anglican Communion meeting in Lambeth Palace." Anglican Communion News Service, October 16, 2003. Online: http://www.anglicannews.org/news/2003/10/a-statement-by-the-primates-of-the-anglican-communion-meeting-in-lambeth-palace.aspx.

Sykes, Stephen, John Booty, and Jonathan Knight, editors. *The Study of Anglicanism*. Rev. ed. Minneapolis: Fortress, 1998.

Virtue, David W. "Pittsburgh Bishop Faces Critical Moment in History." *VirtueOnline*, July 26, 2007. Online: http://www.virtueonline.org/pittsburgh-bishop-faces-critical-moment-history

———. "Pittsburgh Radicals Blast Orthodox Bishop." *VirtueOnline*, May 15, 2004. Online: http://new.virtueonline.org/pittsburgh-radical-media-group-blasts-orthodox-bishop-over-another-bishop.

Wikipedia. "Anglican Province of America. Online: http://en.wikipedia.org/wiki/Anglican_Province_of_America.

Wood, Rodgers T. "An Open Letter to the Bishop and the Bishop Coadjutor of Pittsburgh, in Response to and Support of the Letter from Calvary." Christ Church, Pittsburgh, July 8, 1997. Online: http://theroadtoemmaus.org/RdLb/32Ang/Epis/PghPastLtr.htm.

Zoll, Rachel. "Pittsburgh Episcopal Bishop Robert Duncan Removed by House of Bishops." Associated Press, September 19, 2008. Online: https://episcopalian.wordpress.com/2008/09/19/pittsburgh-episcopal-bishop-robert-duncan-removed-by-house-of-bishops/.